Translated and Edited by Bernard Semmel

WITHDRAWN

Elie Halévy

The Birth
of
Methodism
in
England

The University of Chicago Press
Chicago and London

International Standard Book Number:0-226-31309-3
Libary of Congress Catalog Card Number: 72-131959
The University of Chicago Press, Chicago 60637
The University of Chicago Press, Ltd., London
©1971 by The University of Chicago

The Birth of Methodism
in England

Hanna H. Gray   Advisory Editor
for European History

For M.G.S.
and S.M.S.

Contents

Preface

In translating these articles by Elie Halévy, my object has been to achieve as close a fidelity to Halévy as possible, even to his manner of constructing sentences, that is, to the special flavor of his style, which bears not only Halévy's personal mark, but also that of the period in which he wrote and the scholarly conventions of his country.

In pursuing this object, I have found the suggestions graciously made by Elie Halévy's niece, Dr. Henriette Noufflard Guy-Loé, extremely helpful. Dr. Guy-Loé has also generously made available to me a number of unpublished letters from Halévy's papers which have proved useful in preparing the introduction. I have used the rich pamphlet collections not only of the British Museum, but of the Methodist Archives, The City Road, London, where Dr. J. C. Bowmer proved a most helpful guide to the literature.

Colleagues with whom I have discussed the volume include Professors Gertrude Himmelfarb and Melvin Richter of the City University, R. K. Webb of Columbia University, and W. R. Taylor and David Trask of the State University of New York at Stony Brook. I should like to thank them for their helpful suggestions. I am also appreciative of suggestions made by Professor E. J. Hobsbawm, of Birkbeck College, the University of London. I should like to thank my wife, Maxine, and my students and assistants, Sonia Sbarge, Elizabeth Trask, and Gerard Koot, for typing and related services.

I am particularly grateful to the Guggenheim Foundation for a grant which enabled me to spend a year studying eighteenth-century Methodism.

Bernard Semmel

Stony Brook, Long Island
February 1970

ix

Introduction: Elie Halévy, Methodism, and Revolution

Elie Halévy is perhaps most widely known for the hypothesis, in his classic work *England in 1815*, which suggested that during the years in which the demons of revolution dominated the continent — between, say, 1789 and 1815 — England was spared the revolution toward which the contradictions in her polity and economy might otherwise have led her, through the stabilizing influence of evangelical religion, particularly of Methodism. In the decades following the publication of Halévy's book in 1913, the hypothesis was taken up in one form or another by most of the English historians who addressed themselves to the subject.[1] Halévy's thesis was persuasive to a generation which by endorsing it could indulge in both the sophistication of contemporary German historical sociology — which, following Weber and Troeltsch, saw the importance of ideas, particularly religious ideas, as a shaper of institutions and events — and in a popular Marxism that saw religion as the "opiate of the people." Halévy and his followers were writing at a time when the failure to cite hard evidence was not deemed critical, and it was not until the 1950s that this deficiency was effectively noted.[2] Nevertheless, the thesis continued to be persuasive and maintained its grip on the imagination of historians who began to fill in the evidence.[3]

In recent years, in both England and America, there has been a

1. See, for example, J.L. Hammond and Barbara Hammond, *The Town Labourer, 1760-1832* (London: Longmans, Green, 1917), chaps. 10-12; R.F. Wearmouth, *Methodism and the Common People of the Eighteenth Century* (London: Epworth Press, 1945); and V. Kiernan, "Evangelicalism and the French Revolution," *Past and Present* 1, no. 1 (February 1952): 44-56.

2. See, for example, C.C. Gillispie, "The Work of Elie Halévy: A Critical

1

renewal of interest in eighteenth and nineteenth century English religious history, and, hovering in the background of the efforts to relate religion to social and political issues, the Halévy thesis is almost invariably to be found. Yet the full dimensions of the thesis, as Halévy stated them, have been imperfectly understood. Indeed, the most considerable statement of the thesis by Halévy has gone virtually unread, and the sources of the thesis – a matter of some significance since it does not seem to have emerged from "hard" evidence – have never been explored. If the hypothesis, implicitly or explicitly, is to serve satisfactorily as a stimulus and an instrument of further research, these matters are worth pursuing.

I

Elie Halévy was born in 1870.[4] His great-grandfather had been a cantor of the synagogue service when he had come to Paris from Bavaria toward the end of the eighteenth century. Halévy's grand-

Appreciation," *Journal of Modern History* 22: 232-49; and, in more thorough-going fashion, E.J. Hobsbawm, "Methodism and the Threat of Revolution in Britain," in *Labouring Men: Studies in the History of Labour* (New York: Basic Books, 1964), pp. 23-33. (The article was originally published in *History Today* in 1957.) For another highly critical view of Halévy's ideas concerning Methodism, see J.H.S. Kent, "M. Elie Halévy and Methodism," *Proceedings of the Wesley Historical Society* 29, pt. 4 (December 1953); see also Kent's review in *Proceedings of the Wesley Historical Society* 34, pt. 8 (December 1964): 189.

3. For example, E.P. Thompson, *The Making of the English Working Class* (New York: Pantheon Books, 1964), pp. 41-46, 53-54, 350-51, 355-58, 362-63, 367-70, 375-82, 388-94. See also the discussion in Harold Perkin, *The Origins of Modern English Society, 1780-1880* (London: Routledge and Kegan Paul, 1969), pp. 353-57 and passim.

4. The details of Halévy's life are to be found in L. Brunschvicg, "Elie Halévy (1870-1937)," *Revue de Metaphysique et de Morale* 44, no. 4 (October 1937): 679-92; E. Barker, "Elie Halévy," *English Historical Review* 53, no. 209 (January 1938): 79-87; J.B. Brebner, "Halévy: Diagnostician of Modern Britain," *Thought* 23 no. 88 (March 1948): 101-13; R.K. Webb, "Introduction," to E. Halévy, *The Era of Tyrannies* (New York: Anchor Books, 1965); and most systematically in M. Richter, "Elie Halévy," *International Encyclopedia of the Social Sciences.*

father, Léon, the second son of the Bavarian cantor, became Comte's successor as the secretary of Saint-Simon; Léon's son Ludovic, Elie's father, was the well-known librettist for Offenbach and Bizet. Léon's wife was Catholic, and Ludovic had been raised in that faith. Ludovic married Louise Breguet, of a prominent family of Protestant industrialists, and Elie and Daniel, the sons of this marriage, were raised as Protestants — a matter of some interest to our inquiry. In 1898, Halévy was invited to lecture at the Ecole Libre des Sciences Politiques, founded shortly after France's defeat of 1871 by a group of men seeking to diagnose French instability, which they contrasted with the strength and stability of Victoria's England. For nearly forty years, Halévy was to lecture at the school on the history of European socialism[5] and on modern English history. After the completion of his first book, on Platonic philosophy,[6] Halévy began his work upon Bentham and the philosophical Radicals,[7] an enterprise which brought him to consider subjects beyond the purely metaphysical. It was in the late 1890s that he began making annual visits to England to work at the British Museum or at one of the universities. After his marriage in 1901, his wife, Florence Noufflard, accompanied him on these research expeditions. On his early visits, Halévy was armed with a letter of introduction from Taine, a friend of his father, who had long been associated with the Ecole Libre.

Soon after finishing the *Growth of Philosophic Radicalism,* Halévy turned to consider Methodism, the apparent polar opposite of utilitarianism, though, as he came to believe along with Dicey,[8] its real ally in creating the character of modern England. Halévy con-

---

5. A volume of student notes of these lectures was published as E. Halévy, *Histoire du socialisme européen* (Paris: Gallimard, 1948).

6. *La théorie platonicienne des sciences* (Paris: Felix Alcan, 1896).

7. *La formation du radicalisme philosophique* (Paris: Felix Alcan, 1901-04), translated as *The Growth of Philosophic Radicalism* (London, 1928).

8. See A.V. Dicey, *Lectures on the Relation between Law and Public Opinion in England during the Nineteenth Century* (London: Macmillan, 1914), pp. 400-09.

fessed himself an unbeliever who regarded Buddhism as coming closest to truth;[9] yet his Protestant background, in particular the strong influence of his mother, helped to endow him with a sympathy for the subject of Methodism, upon which he began serious research in the summer of 1905. "I am going to the other side of the Channel," he wrote to a friend, Célestin Bouglé, on 4 July 1905, "to cultivate my garden and to study Methodism, just as I would," he added (no doubt to reassure his friend concerning a possible outcropping of religiosity!), "Buddhism or Babism."[10] On 31 July, he wrote to another friend, Xavier Léon, from Oxford that he was working "very fruitfully," and had already discovered masses of material which no one had used previously. The core of his work, he observed, was "to define those two forms of Christian religious exaltation which are called Catholicism and Protestantism"; strangely enough, Halévy wrote, no one had ever attempted to do this.[11] A month later, on 27 August, Halévy wrote to Léon again, this time from Penzance. Before leaving Oxford, Halévy had discovered that a "Normalien"[12] had already been at work for some time on Wesley and English Methodism. "I have learned this two months or even a year too late," he observed sadly.[13] A couple of weeks later, in a letter to Bouglé, he remarked that he had "always contemplated a History of England in the Nineteenth Century" and that the notes would prove useful in that enterprise.[14] Clearly, however, Halévy wished to make more direct and immediate use of the material he had gathered, and in the following August two articles entitled "La naissance du

9. See Alain [A. Chartier], *Correspondance avec Elie et Florence Halévy* (Paris: Gallimard, 1958), p. 325.

10. Ibid., p. 331.

11. Ibid., p. 332.

12. The "Normalien" was Augustin Léger (see unpublished letter of Halévy to Bouglé, 30 July 1905, in the possession of Dr. H. Noufflard Guy-Loé) whose program of research was to prove very different from Halévy's. See Augustin Léger, *L'Angleterre religieuse et les origines du Méthodisme au XVIIIe siècle; la jeunesse de Wesley* (Paris, Hachette, 1910).

13. Alain, *Correspondance*, p. 332.

14. Ibid., pp. 332-33.

Méthodisme en Angleterre" appeared in the *Revue de Paris*.[15] Although these articles are known — Halévy referred to them in a footnote in *England in 1815*[16] — they seem to have been virtually unread in the English-speaking world;[17] it must be presumed that their relative inaccessibility or their not having been translated are responsible for this neglect.

Historians had tried "to dramatize" the revival, Halévy observed in the first of these articles, by suggesting that the preaching of Wesley and Whitefield had transformed a country in which "absolute irreligion and immorality" reigned to one which enjoyed "universal exaltation." As usual, "the truth is less simple." The contrast frequently made between a "clerical" France and an "irreligious" England was a false one. Seventeeth-century Puritanism had "left deep marks on the popular consciousness." It had produced the "grave, reserved, silent, and melancholy" Englishman in whose very tolerance there was "hidden a kind of religiosity," a sense of awe at the "incomprehensible mystery" of the universe, which constituted "the mystic foundation of English liberalism." On the other hand, the "frivolousness" of the Frenchman proved more useful for "the temperament of the freethinker," and French rationalism seemed less conducive to the promotion of tolerance. Although the propagation of irreligious ideas in England was undoubtedly making the English less melancholy and less theological, Halévy pointed to the formation within Anglicanism of "numerous and flourishing" voluntary societies to combat vice, and religious societies to "enlighten the faithful" — among them the society set up by the Wesleys at Oxford in 1729 — to prove that the "decline of the religious spirit" had been exaggerated. The Dissenting sects had, indeed, been in

15. 1 and 15 August, 1906, pp. 519-39, and 841-67.

16. Vol. 1, p. 368n of the original edition (Paris: Hachette, 1912), refers incorrectly to the dates of the articles as 15 August and 1 September. The English translation (London: E. Benn, 1949) repeats this error, p. 389n.

17. C.C. Gillispie, in the article cited earlier, is one exception; for another, see John Walsh, "Origins of the Evangelical Revival," in G.V. Bennett and J.D. Walsh, *Essays in Modern English Church History, in Memory of Norman Sykes* (London: A. & C. Black, 1966), p. 132.

decline since 1688 due to the increasing liberalism and rationalism of the Dissenting ministers, in some cases deserting their flocks for Anglicanism or Socinianism; but the rank and file of Dissent cleaved to the old faith. The reservoir of Protestant emotions of the Dissenting faithful, which their own ministers were unable or unwilling to tap, was plumbed to the depths by the Methodists, who combined "the ecclesiastical zeal" of the High Church clergy and societies with "the Protestant piety of the mass of the faithful." The great accomplishment of Wesley and Whitefield was not that of creating "a completely new initiative," as it were "ex nihilo." Rather they brought together "well-defined, preexisting elements" in "a new combination."

The High Church societies were not able to bring forth the revival on their own, Halévy suggested, because "the Protestant, or Puritan impulse failed them." It was only after their conversion to the authentic Protestantism of salvation by faith that John Wesley and his Methodists were able "to act upon the consciousness of the nation." The German Moravian missonaries of Count Zinzendorf, first in Georgia, and then in London, were primarily responsible for this conversion. Methods of evangelizing which could only have been either "unknown or repugnant" to ordained ministers of the Church of England, as both Whitefield and Wesley were, would have to be employed; such methods had been developed by Griffith Jones and Howell Harris, in a still almost barbaric Wales. Barred from preaching in the churches, first Whitefield and then Wesley emulated these methods and, by their preaching in the fields, succeeded in producing feelings of extreme exaltation on the part of their listeners. Without the conversion to Protestantism and the imitation of the preaching of the Welsh revivalists, the "popular revolution" which was Methodism could not have occurred.

The preaching of Wesley and Whitefield, moreover, "encountered favorable conditions"; at the very time of this revival "a political revolution was underway," closely related to the religious revolution. In 1738, Halévy noted, Walpole was faced with an imposing parliamentary opposition supported by growing public discontent, and found himself compelled to make war with both France and

Spain. How was this "political revolution" to be explained? Halévy suggested that the "industrial era" had begun at about 1688, and he viewed the period of the great inventions, in the last decades of the eighteenth century, as resting upon a considerable anterior industrial development. The regime of "manufacture" during the early part of the eighteenth century displayed, Halévy argued, a number of the characteristics usually regarded as belonging exclusively to that of "machinofacture." There was pauperism in all the industrial centers − especially in the villages of Wiltshire and Yorkshire − just as there would be in the industrial cities a century later, and with pauperism was associated "the ignorance, immorality, and intemperance" of the working classes. Toward the end of the 1730s, a commercial crisis took place. It was, Halévy asserted, a crisis of overproduction, which is generally believed not to have occurred until "the increase of mechanization increased the volume of production." This crisis brought about the fall of Walpole's policy of peace, for England's merchants, manufacturers, and shipowners − finding "the disposal of their products difficult" and galled by Spain's interference with their ships in her effort to safeguard her trade monopoly − became "restless and provocative." Pitt was the spokesman for this new mood. Walpole's policy of "moral and religious skepticism" was also in jeopardy, when "the bestial state to which the lower classes had been reduced" was revealed by the disturbances produced by the crisis.

This same economic crisis, Halévy observed, "spurred the eruption of Methodism." Noting that the times and places where "the industrial crisis" was the most severe were identical with the times and places where "the religious crisis" was most evident, Halévy had no doubt but that "the two crises are tied together." It was in the region south of Bristol from the Atlantic to the English Channel, then the center of the woolen industry, that the distress was keenest and the agitation and rioting of the working classes greatest. Sectarian Protestantism had long been influential in the area, and with the onset of troubles "it was but natural that Christian enthusiasm endeavored to turn this popular ferment to its own profit." Here Wesley and Whitefield and their early disciples first came to preach in the fields: "the despair of the working class was the raw material to which Methodist doctrine and discipline gave a shape." The same crisis hit the industrial villages of Yorkshire and helped to "generate" a revival there. In Yorkshire, just as in the Bristol region, hunger and high wheat prices had led to arson, pillage, and rioting, all "favorable circumstances for the progress of religious exaltation." Distress and Methodism spread together among the miners of Cornwall and Wales, through the Midlands and Lancashire. The efforts of Wesley and Whitefield understandably gave rise to fears of a renewal of the revolutionary feelings associated with the religious enthusiasm of the preceding century. But Methodism was clearly not "a revolutionary or a communist doctrine," and these early fears were soon allayed.

Why, Halévy asked, did the working-class agitation of 1738, "after its violent beginnings," take the "form of a religious and mystical movement" whose ideal was "extremely conservative, rather than terminating in a social revolution?" Halévy saw the problem as posing difficulties only "insofar as one has illusions concerning the role that the common people play in history." The answer, for Halévy, lay in the role of that "singularly influential class" the bourgeoisie, those who occupied "posts of command, high or low, in the economy." The proletariat, accessible as it was to "the prompt contagion of all violent emotions," could not by itself decide on the direction of its enthusiasm; it looked to the bourgeoisie for "a doctrine, an ideal." If, in 1739, there had been a bourgeoisie "moved by revolutionary sentiments and convinced that it must instigate a movement of intimidation and insurrection" so as to satisfy its demands, it would at that time have "been able to bring about a democratic social revolution"; but the English bourgeoisie was not revolutionary, or republican — remembering as it did "the horror" of the Civil Wars — nor was it irreligious. When economic crisis provided "the raw material for a general revolt," the "popular discontent took the form that the discontent of the bourgeoisie wished to give it, a religious and conservative form." This was the case in 1739, Halévy declared, and it continued to be so into the twentieth century.

Even today, whenever a Methodist preacher brings a popular
audience together at a street corner to read the Bible, sing
hymns, and pray in common, whenever he induces a "revival"
of mysticism and religious exaltation, in a region or throughout the nation, the great movement of 1739 is being repeated,
in the pattern fixed by tradition, with climactic changes of
mood that everybody — passionate participants and disinterested spectators — can foresee in advance. A force capable
of expending itself in displays of violence or popular upheavals,
assumes, under the influence of a century and a half of
Methodism, the form least capable of unsettling a social order
founded upon inequality of rank and wealth.

This was why, Halévy concluded, modern England possessed no genuine "parties of social and political revolution," and why England
has remained a "Puritan nation."

In these terms Halévy depicted the sociopsychological dynamic
by which Methodism — as well as the Dissenting sects and the
Church of England, which were transformed by Methodist evan-
gelism — made its great, direct contribution to English stability in
the nineteenth century. The structure in which the dynamic was set
forth was hardly free of flaws. One might ask, for example, how necessary the "crisis of overproduction" was to Halévy's picture of 1739;
would not great and widespread distress have been sufficient for his
purposes? There are other grounds for debate. The most controver-
sial part of the articles was Halévy's projection of the Methodist
achievement in blocking revolution in 1739 to the subsequent history of England. Here was the preparation for the statement of his
position in *England in 1815.*

In 1896, while still at work upon his book on Benthamism and
before beginning his study of Methodism, Halévy pondered whether
he should next undertake "a theory of society, a theory of modern
democracy, or a history of England?"[18] It was to the last subject, as
we know, that Halévy was ultimately called. *England in 1815,* a
masterpiece of European historiography, appeared in 1913. The

18. Alain, *Correspondance,* p. 325.

book, embracing all of Halévy's three possibilities, bears the mark of the primacy of Halévy's philosophic interests, the predominance of the intellectual historian in his makeup. "Why was it," Halévy inquired in this volume, "that of all the countries of Europe England has been the most free from revolutions, violent crises, and sudden changes?" Was it because of her Constitution, her political system? The British constitution was "anarchic," and the government had been "systematically weakened, always a prey to internal strife, and deprived by the Constitution itself of the necessary means to repress economic or religious disorders, the war of classes and creeds." Was it because of England's comparative freedom, as an island, from the menace of a continental invader? Was it, as Tocqueville had earlier suggested, the absence of a centralized bureaucracy of which a revolutionary minority might seize control? Halévy regarded such explanations as "insufficient." Was the secret of England's stability to be found in her economic system? Hardly. There had been serious industrial crises, accompanied by business failures, unemployment, starvation; workers "imbued with revolutionary ideas" rioted; there was "open war" between urban Free Traders and the Protectionists of the countryside. Sismondi, who had visited England in 1817, had been "terrified by the spectacle of revolution," which he regarded as inevitable under the prevailing economic system. Even Ricardo saw class wars as inescapable, and a generation later Marx, availing himself of the insights of Sismondi and Ricardo, had no doubt that the industrial revolution, with its attendant miseries, must end in a liberating social revolution. "If the materialist interpretation of history is to be trusted," Halévy observed, "if economic facts explain the course taken by the human race in its progress, the England of the nineteenth century was surely, above all countries, destined to revolution, both political and religious." But, Halévy added, "it was not to be so."

But why not? Halévy resumed the terms of analysis of his 1906 articles. England's "political institutions were such," he argued, "that society might easily have lapsed into anarchy had there existed in England a bourgeoisie animated by the spirit of revolution"; the system of economic production was so anarchic as to have "plunged the kingdom into violent revolution" if the working classes had found middle-class leaders able to provide them with "a definite ideal, a creed, a practical program." "But the élite of the working class, the hardworking and capable bourgeois, had been imbued by the evangelical movement with a spirit from which the established order had nothing to fear." This spirit — conservative and antirevolutionary — derived from the Methodist revival of the previous century. Methodism had brought under its influence the Dissenters, the Establishment, and finally even "secular opinion." The Revival had stimulated an Evangelical movement within the Church of England, and it was to these Evangelicals that the reform of the "national morality" was largely due; it was they who exercised upon the upper classes, most particularly after the French Revolution had displayed the fruits of irreligion, "a direct influence akin to that exercised by the Methodists on the masses." Indeed, England at this time believed that her victory in 1815 stemmed from her cultivation of "moral qualities" which the French lacked, and in the century which followed, evangelical opinion helped to enforce laws against blasphemy, drunkenness, and obscenity, and ensured that the Sabbath would be a day of rest. This last was advocated to employers as helping to produce, in Halévy's words, "a religious and obedient proletariat." Here was the source of "the miracle of modern England, anarchist but orderly, practical and business-like, but religious and even pietist." While defending liberty in the form of that "freedom of association" without which they themselves could not exist, the sects, in association with the forces of authority, imposed on the nation "a rigorous ethical conformity and at least an outward respect for the Christian social order." "With their passion for liberty they united a devotion to order," Halévy observed, "and in the last resort the latter predominated."

These efforts were largely made not by the state but by voluntary associations, lacking powers of "legal coercion," and consequently obliged to establish "a powerful moral authority alike over their own members and over society as a whole." Such voluntary associations, Halévy continued, moral and religious, philanthropic and scientific, are an outstanding characteristic of modern England. They "fashioned the character of the English middle class" — "dogmatic in morals, proud of its practical outlook, and sufficiently powerful to obtain respect for its views from the proletariat . . . [and] from the aristocracy." The source of all this was in Methodism and its organization. "Methodism was the antidote to Jacobinism," Halévy declared in the concluding paragraph of *England in 1815;* "the free organization of the sects was the foundation of social order in England." England was a free country because, "at bottom," England was "a country of voluntary obedience, of an organization freely initiated and freely accepted."[19]

This, then, was the shape that Halévy's view of Methodism assumed when it appeared as the dominating theme of *England in 1815.* We must stress that Halévy, like Max Weber at about the same time, was not, as is frequently believed, attempting to replace an economic interpretation by an idealistic interpretation of history. Halévy, like Weber, was suspicious of all efforts to understand history as the product of a single cause, and he saw religion as capable of altering what appeared to be the otherwise almost "inevitable" tendency of the internal contradictions (as both Ricardo and Marx understood them) of the new industrialism to produce revolution. Nor did Halévy fail to stress — and this is a matter which many of his critics neglect — that, while Methodism was the grand source of the crucial religious influence, that influence was exerted, in the main, indirectly, by the infiltration of the Methodist spirit into the ranks of the Dissenters and, through the Evangelicals, into the Established Church, and by the imposition of a new morality upon *all* classes by means of the activities of voluntary associations.

II

In his 1906 articles, Halévy spoke of it as being "generally agreed" that Methodism had contributed to "preventing the French Revolution from having an English counterpart." Certainly, very early in

19. *England in 1815* (English ed.) pp. 200, 382-83, 387, 389-90, 410, 415, 417, 419, 421, 423-28, 433-34, 450-51, 451-52, 590-91.

the nineteenth century, it was not unusual to consider Wesley and Voltaire the two antipodal figures of the previous century, with the implication that the latter had helped to make, and the former to prevent, a revolution. Southey's two-volume work on Wesley, for example, was couched in such terms.[20] In France, a tradition of contrasting French and English development had long existed. Montesquieu and Voltaire had founded it, and differences in religious attitudes had attracted their considerable interest. Tocqueville wrote much of his *Ancien Régime and the French Revolution* with England, and more particularly England's freedom from revolution, in mind.[21] Guizot, probably France's greatest historian in the mid-nineteenth century, and a Protestant, proclaimed that "never was the author of a great and durable popular movement farther removed from any revolutionary tendency than was Wesley." Moreover, Wesley and Methodism were "to reanimate the moral element in England, to purify her manners, and give her strength to resist the fatal allurement of the French Revolution."[22] Others, like the Comte de Rémusat and Matthieu Lelièvre, echoed Guizot and came near to Halévy's subsequent formulation.[23]

Halévy was, no doubt, familiar with many of these earlier views — which rarely rose above the level of simple assertion — but he appears to have been especially under the influence of Hippolyte Taine, who was, as noted, a family friend. The influence of Taine upon Halévy's entire *oeuvre* must be stressed. It was, as Brunschvicg

20. Voltaire, wrote Southey, was "the arch-infidel," whose teachings had "brought down the whole fabric of government in France, overturned her altars, subverted her throne, carried guilt, devastation, and misery into every part of his own country, and shook the rest of Europe like an earthquake"; on the other hand, Southey observed, "Wesley's doctrines, meantime, were slowly and gradually winning their way . . . and their effect must ultimately be more extensive, more powerful, and more permanent, for he had set mightier principles at work." R. Southey, *The Life of Wesley and the Rise and Progress of Methodism* (London: Longman, 1820), 1:2-3.

21. See S.I. Drescher, *Tocqueville and England* (Cambridge, Mass.: Harvard University Press, 1964), passim.

22. Guizot, *A Popular History of England* (Boston, 1876), 4:185-87.

23. See, for example, C. de Rémusat, *De la Réforme et du Protestantisme*

observed, Taine's program for the discussion of modern French history that Halévy was to apply to England.[24] Taine, however, more the essayist, had embroidered in splendid, rhetorical fashion only upon leading themes, while Halévy played the role of the historian to whom nothing was alien. Yet, if Taine's magnum opus, *Les origines de la France contemporaine,* was the model for Halévy's *History,* no reader of the first volume of Taine's work, that on the ancien régime, can fail to see how Halévy's *England in 1815* followed its example, particularly in the role Halévy assigned to the Methodist hypothesis. It should be noted also that Taine, in his *History of English Literature,* published more than forty years before the appearance of Halévy's articles, had discussed Methodism in very much the same terms that Halévy was to employ. Indeed, in Taine's lengthy contrast between the seeming and the real differences in English and French religiosity at the beginning of the eighteenth century, we see, almost allusion for allusion, hints of the early sections of Halévy's first article: the contrast between the supposed irreligiosity of England and "the moral sense" of the English; the view of the Englishman as "naturally serious, meditative, and sad," whose eyes were turned "inward to the life of the soul"; the view that such a temperament gave "a support to Protestantism," and gave the Englishman a religious frame of mind; that beneath an apparent irreligiosity, "the cooled Puritan spirit still broods under-

---

(Paris, 1854), pp. 55-56, where Rémusat sees Protestantism as a better defense against socialism, the new Jacobinism, than Catholicism. Matthieu Lelièvre, a French Methodist pastor, in his biography of Wesley gave full credits, as Halévy was to do, to the Evangelicals, as well as to the Methodists, noting that "in the working classes, men but lately ungovernable became, under the influence of evangelical preaching, steady and industrious." The Awakening had been "a great revolution," Lelièvre had concluded, which "following on the heels of the political Revolution" of the century earlier, had created "modern England, that nation which has set the world an example of the power and permanence of liberal institutions based on the foundation of the gospel." M. Lelièvre, *John Wesley: His Life and Work* (London: C.H. Kelly, 1900), pp. 470-73.

24. "Elie Halévy," pp. 684-85.

ground." For Taine — as later for Halévy — Wesley and Whitefield typified the English character. "In spite of Hume and Voltaire, they founded a monastic and convulsionary sect, and triumphed through austerity and exaggeration, which would have ruined them in France." It was they who rallied "round Christianity all the forces which in France Voltaire ranges against it." Indeed, "they all defend it on the same ground — as a tie for civil society and a support for private virtue." Taine's conclusion — in line with those of Southey, Rémusat, and Guizot — was that "thus Englishmen arrive on the threshold of the French Revolution, conservatives and Christians facing the French freethinkers and revolutionaries."[25] In his *Notes on England,* published in the 1860s, Taine displayed a similar awareness of the importance of the role played by Evangelicalism in creating modern England, and he also noted the special role of voluntary, private associations.[26] Taine in his youth had been the special protégé of Guizot, and we might almost trace the succession of Guizot to Taine to Halévy — two of them raised as Protestants — all seeking the answer to the same question and emerging with the same general reply: that England's freedom from revolution lay in the influence of Methodism.

Many works appeared in France in the last decades of the nineteenth century which addressed themselves to the causes of the French Revolution. Historians like Rocquain and Aubertin saw the cause in a political breakdown arising from the struggles of the king and the *parlements;* Champion saw economic grievances as foremost; Faguet agreed, and spoke of a general governmental breakdown. Lanson and, more particularly, Taine, in the tradition of the Conservative theorists de Maistre and de Bonald, believed it was the *philosophes* who had produced the Revolution. The first volume of Taine's *Origines* speaks of the "chimera" born of "the catechism of the rights of man, and other dogmas of anarchical and despotic character," becoming "a raging, formidable brute"; "they have had

25. H.A. Taine, *History of English Literature* (Edinburgh, 1874) 3:71-85, 90-91, 92, 95-99, 118, 141-42.

26. *Notes on England* (Fair Lawn, N.J.: Essential Books, 1958), pp. 156-85 and passim.

the doctrine preached to them that they are sovereign, and they act as sovereigns"; "the condition of their intellects being given, nothing is more natural than their conduct"; "the upper class disarmed by its very humanity"; the "nightmare" of irreligion and democracy; "several millions of savages are thus let loose by a few thousand declaimers."[27] What would be more natural, then, for Halévy, who drew the plans of his *History* about the theme of why England did *not* have a revolution, to turn, in discounting the view that English stability was a product of her political or economic institutions, to the realm of ideas? To a trained philosopher and a historian of thought, the prospect could only be congenial; in his later analysis of the origins of the first World War, Halévy was to announce that he was "no believer in the materialist conception of history" and that it was idealism which made revolutions and wars.[28] Halévy's study of utilitarianism, however, had proved to him that philosophical radicalism, taken by itself, *had* all the revolutionary potential of French philosophic thought. The Methodist thesis had already been sketched out by Halévy's French predecessors, as we have observed, and Halévy became convinced that it was the solution to his problem.

In this instance, it is probably necessary to dispute Brunschvicg's view of Halévy's method of not "avoir trouvé avant d'avoir cherché."[29] The very existence of the articles before Halévy had begun the detailed studies which produced *England in 1815* suggests a *parti pris,* at least so far as the later period is concerned; and Taine's role in providing Halévy with that *parti pris,* even for the earlier period, seems to have been substantial. Guizot had made a simple assertion; Taine had placed it in the impressionistic but persuasive, literary setting of a contrast of national characters, which Halévy was to imitate in his first article for the *Revue de Paris;* and, as we have noted, the structure of the first volume of Taine's *Origines,* given Halévy's turn of mind, could not fail to exert a

27. Taine, *The Ancient Régime* (New York: Henry Holt, 1896), pp. 396-97, 399.
28. *Era of Tyrannies,* pp. 224, and passim.
29. "Elie Halévy," p. 685.

powerful influence upon the structure of the first volume of Halévy's *History*. Halévy, then, was moving within a well-marked tradition of French sociological history. If he required any further confirmation of this *parti pris*, one perhaps better grounded in historical fact than those offered by his other predecessors, it was provided by W. E. H. Lecky in his seven-volume *History of England in the Eighteenth Century*, published in the last quarter of the nineteenth century.

Lecky's work, to which Halévy was to refer in both the 1906 articles and in *England in 1815*, lifted the level of discussion of the Methodist hypothesis beyond that of simple assertion; yet his view was supported by little more evidence than Southey had provided some generations earlier. Lecky had no doubt about the importance of the "religious revolution" that the Wesleys and Whitefield had ushered in, and of the influence of the evangelical movement, which "more or less permeated every section of society." The revolt conducted by Voltaire and the Encyclopaedists against the supernatural theory of Christianity, the materialism of Condillac and Helvétius, the "wild social dreams" of Rousseau, "had together produced in France a revolutionary spirit, which in its intensity and its proselytising fervour was unequalled since the days of the Reformation." The spirit — "which could only lead to anarchy, and at length to despotism" and was "fatal to that measured and ordered freedom which can alone endure" — spread. England, almost alone, "escaped the contagion." "Many causes conspired to save her," but a prominent place among them, Lecky believed, had to be given to the "religious enthusiasm" then "passing through the middle and lower classes of the people, which had enlisted in its services a large proportion of the wilder and more impetuous reformers, and which recoiled with horror from the anti-Christian tenets that were associated with the Revolution in France." Lecky then turned to certain of the consequences of the growth of industry in England at this time, the "breaking the ties of sympathy between class and class, and destroying the habits of discipline and subordination that once extended through the whole community." All this produced "a restless discontent"; "the inflammable elements in the nation were massed together to an unprecedented extent"; "the war between capital and labour began" as "the contrast between extravagant luxury and abject misery" became "more frequent" and "more glaring." "It is, therefore, I conceive," Lecky concluded, "peculiarly fortunate" that this great increase in manufacturing "should have been preceded by a religious revival, which opened a new spring of moral and religious energy among the poor, and at the same time gave a powerful impulse to the philanthropy of the rich."[30]

Halévy was clearly not obliged to take a leap into the dark. It might be said of Halévy and the Methodist thesis what Halévy said of Wesley and Methodism: Halévy's great accomplishment was not that of creating "a completely new initiative," as it were "ex nihilo," but of bringing together "well-defined, preexisting elements" in a "new combination."

III

The debate concerning Methodism and revolution with which we have become familiar in the last decade and a half began, perhaps surprisingly, in the quarter of a century before Waterloo. From its earliest days, as is well known, Methodism had appeared to many in both state and church to be posing the clear threat of revolution. It seemed to be a revival of the enthusiasm and the antinomianism of the seventeenth century. The government had, in the decades which followed the onset of the Revival, been reassured by the steadfast loyalty of John Wesley, a good Tory who, almost uniquely among the Dissenters, had even defended Lord North against the American revolutionists. Nevertheless, leaders of the Methodist Connection were always aware that the government — as a consequence of the intermittent agitation of clergymen and prelates of the Church of England and the concern felt in high political places about the potential danger of a fanatical, sectarian mass movement in times of national distress — might find it useful to restrain the spread of

30. W.E.H. Lecky, *A History of England in the Eighteenth Century* (London: Longmans, Green, 1878-90), 2:611, 634-38.

Methodism or even to suppress it entirely. After Wesley's death in 1791, no doubt in response to the unrest produced by events in France, charges that Methodism was potentially revolutionary came up with increasing frequency. Fears of Methodism became sharp in the mid-1790s as an egalitarian minority of Methodists fought to democratize the government of the Connection. Many politicians and Anglican clergymen and prelates reacted with paranoia at the prospect of over a hundred thousand Methodists, under the tight discipline of a central committee of one hundred which dispatched scores of itinerant preachers throughout the kingdom to guide hundreds of chapels. Nor was it an unnatural fear, for the Methodists were the only body of the "people" who were so organized as to be capable of making a revolution. Moreover, the expansive energies of Methodism appeared to be at their height, and Methodism, having devoted its attentions for half a century to the proletariat in the mines and the new industrial towns, was turning its attention to the previously unassailed rural districts, heretofore the acknowledged monopoly of the Established Church.

The Anglican clergy and bishops took alarm. They feared the "leveling" principle in the Methodist system of lay preaching; they dreaded the fanaticism of the converted. Some saw a revolutionary conspiracy being hatched by the Connection. In 1807, the Bishop of Gloucester, an Evangelical but an enemy of the Methodists, depicted the Establishment as a "citadel" which was "beset on every side" by Methodists "who wish not well to the civil and religious polity of this nation." These "malignant and subtle adversaries," through "their private conferences, their local classes, their extensive connections, their general assemblies . . . cooperate from one part of the Kingdom to another . . . for the purpose of concerting measures to undermine our civil and religious Constitution." More and more, the Anglican critics of Methodists were inquiring whether Methodists, with their peculiar system of itinerancy and their uncertain status as Dissenters, ought to be protected by the Toleration Acts.[31]

Methodist leaders continued to insist, as Wesley had done, that

31. G.I. Huntingford, Bishop of Gloucester, *A Charge Delivered to the Clergy of the Diocese of Gloucester* (London: Cadell & Davies, 1807), pp.

their allegiance to the king and his government was a spiritual imperative. This was the usual Tory appeal to divine right and passive obedience, loyalty to the monarch "not only for wrath but for conscience's sake."[32] From the 1790s onward they also insisted, anticipating the earliest historiographical formulation of what we call the Halévy thesis, that if England was not being assailed by revolutionary demons as France was, this was attributable to the stabilizing influence of Methodism. This theme was repeated again and again in Methodist sermons which assumed that, not only was Methodism in good part responsible for spawning Britain's new industrial growth, but it was the means by which "vast groups of loose and disorderly men, subject as they have been to sudden stoppages in trade, to exorbitant advances of provisions, have been governed almost without mobbing and confusion." No longer were there "very serious riots among colliers and manufacturers" as in times past.[33]

The frequency and intensity of both the Anglican accusations and the Methodist defenses appear to have reached a climax when, in 1811, the Home Secretary, Lord Sidmouth, introduced a bill in the House of Lords to defend the interests of the Establishment against the expansion of Methodism. The bill, seemingly a comparatively mild

22-23, 26, 29-30. See also George Croft, D.D., *Thoughts Concerning the Methodists and the Established Clergy* (London: Rivington, 1795), pp. 49-50; and Anon., *A Letter to a Country Gentleman, on the Subject of Methodism . . . from the Clergyman of His Parish* (Ipswich, 1805), pp. 18, 19 n., 20, 21, 23-25, 31, 33, 41 n., 41-42.

32. For examples of this argument, see Samuel Bradburn, *Methodism Set Forth and Defended in a Sermon . . . Preached at the Opening of Portland Chapel, Bristol, August 26, 1792* (Bristol: Lancaster and Edwards, 1792), pp. 51-52; and Joseph Benson, *A Defence of the Methodists in Five Letters Addressed to the Rev. Dr. Tatham* (London, 1793), pp. 42, 58.

33. Joseph Sutcliffe, *A Review of Methodism* (York: Wilson and Spence, 1805), pp. 37-38. See also Thomas Taylor, *Britannia's Mercies, and her Duty; Considered in Two Discourses delivered in the Methodist Chapel, at Halifax . . . November 29, 1798* (Leeds, 1799), pp. 29-30; and John Pawson, *The Prophet's Advice to the People of God in the Time of Danger. Sermon . . . Preached in the Methodist Chapel, in London . . . 1799* (Leeds: E. Baines, 1801), pp. 11, 18-19, 22-24.

attempt to correct "abuses" in the Acts of Toleration and to place certain obstacles in the way of lay preaching, was received by the Methodists (and by the Dissenters who rushed to their support) as the opening wedge of an effort to destroy the Connection, and to wage a new war against Dissent generally. The Whigs in the Upper House — among them Lords Holland, Stanhope, Grey, and Erskine — attacked Sidmouth's bill in this spirit and defended the Methodists.[34] Although Sidmouth had not accused the Methodists of revolutionary designs, many of the supporters of his proposed legislation outside of parliament had no doubt that the Methodists were "the pious champions" of Jacobinism, who had "decreed the subversion of all the established religions in the world" and whose "real object" was revolution.[35] To counter Sidmouth's efforts, hundreds of petitions were assembled in a wonderfully short time by a joint committee of Methodists and the three principal Dissenting denominations.[36] Rebutting the enemies of the Connection, the Methodists saw the effect of their revival as "raising the standard of public morals, and in promoting loyalty in the middle ranks, as well as subordination and industry in the lower orders of Society."[37]

34. *Parliamentary Debates,* House of Lords, XIX, 9 May 1811, pp. 1128-34.

35. *Mr. Redhead Yorke's Weekly Political Review,* 25 May 1811, pp. 353-54; see also pp. 355 ff. Cobbett, on the other hand, writing in 1811 as a convert to Jacobinism, denounced the Methodists as enemies to change. See *Cobbett's Weekly Political Register* (London), 25 May 1811, pp. 1283-84, 1293.

36. See Maldwyn Edwards, *After Wesley: A Study of the Social and Political Influence of Methodism in the Middle Period (1791-1849)* (London: Epworth Press, 1948), pp. 75-78.

37. *A Narrative of the Proceedings of the General Committee of the People Called Methodists, Late in Connexion with the Rev. John Wesley; Of Protestant Dissenters, and other Friends to Religious Liberty, Respecting the Bill, Introduced into the House of Lords, by Lord Viscount Sidmouth* etc. (London: For Methodist Preaching Houses, 1811), pp. 13-15. See also *Resolutions of the Methodist Ministers of the Manchester District, Assembled at Liverpool, 23 May 1811, on the subject of a Bill Introduced into Parliament by the Rt. Hon Lord Viscount Sidmouth* etc. (Liverpool: Kaye, 1811), pp. 3-4.

Sidmouth, after the storm of petitions and Whig defenses of the Toleration Acts, was urged by a cabinet colleague, Lord Liverpool, by the Archbishop of Canterbury, and by the Lord Chancellor to withdraw his bill. He was at first reluctant to do so. In the debate which followed, not only were the protections afforded by the Toleration Acts extolled, but encomiums were bestowed on the Methodists "for the rectitude of their lives and abstinence from political affairs." Under such pressures, the bill was doomed.[38] In the months ahead, in courts throughout the country there was a rash of cases in which Methodist itinerants were brought before the magistrates and asked to prove themselves the teacher or preacher of some particular congregation, and, if unable to do so, they were refused permission to preach. The Methodists were disturbed that certain sections of the press had labeled them *"vermin fit only to be destroyed,"* and that parliament was "loudly and repeatedly called upon to adopt measures of coercion" against them, "under the pretence that evangelical religion was inimical to public security and morals."[39] It was in such a climate of opinion that the Methodists petitioned for and received protection from the new prime minister, Lord Liverpool, in July 1812. Both the Conventicle Act and the Five Mile Act were repealed. Stanhope and Holland applauded the prime minister, while Sidmouth offered grudging approval.[40]

The preachers assembled at the annual Methodist Conference in 1812 thanked those who had given them their support, and expressed their confidence that they owed this great boon to their "well-known loyalty," "their dutiful attachment to their King and

---

38. *Parliamentary Debates,* House of Lords XX, 21 May 1811, pp. 233-55; 17 May 1811, pp. 196-98. See also Thomas Roberts, *The Outcasts Delivered etc.* (Camarthen: Harris, 1811), with its grateful dedication to Lord Erskine for opposing Sidmouth's Bill.

39. *Minutes of the Methodist Conferences, from the First Held in London by the Late Rev. John Wesley, A.M., in the Year 1744* (London: John Mason, at the Wesleyan Conference Office, 1862). 3 (1812): 308-9.

40. *Parliamentary Debates,* House of Lords, XXIII, 23 July 1812, pp. 1191-93; see also 2 June 1812, pp. 318-19; 3 July 1812, pp. 887-92; House of Commons, XXIII, 21 July 1812, pp. 1108-9.

Country, and the simplicity and purity of their object in promoting their own salvation, and that of others." The confidence in Methodism displayed by the government, the address observed, "strengthens our motives for obedience."[41] The Methodist leadership regarded the result of parliamentary inaction in 1811 and of parliamentary action in 1812 to have settled the question concerning Methodism and revolution. In 1813, a Methodist itinerant, denying still another accusation that Methodism was a revival of a rebellious Puritanism, not only countered, in the usual fashion, that the Methodists had contributed to the "industry, sobriety, good order and moral decorum" of the lower classes, but added that "the arguments offered on this head in the House of Lords by those illustrious peers who opposed Lord Sidmouth's bill were incapable of being controverted." Moreover, he added, the circumstances under which the 1812 legislation was passed proved that the government was satisfied with "the peaceable and loyal conduct of the Methodists."[42] Other Methodist preachers followed the same reasoning.[43] The High Court of Parliament, the Methodists and Dissenters appear to have believed, had weighed the arguments of three-quarters of a century and had decided that far from being fomenters of revolution, as their enemies had repeatedly charged, the Methodists were in the van of those who were contributing to the stability of society in a revolutionary age.

41. *Address of the Preachers Assembled at the Sixty-Ninth Annual Conference, Begun in Leeds, July 27, 1812, to the Members of the Methodist Societies Founded by the late Rev. John Wesley* (n.p.: Conference Office, 1812), pp. 1,2.

42. John Hughes, *A Plea for Religious Liberty; Or a Vindication of the Methodists: To Which is Subjoined the Controversy between the Author and Civis in the Macclesfield Courier* (Macclesfield, 1813), pp. iv-v, 8-9.

43. See, for example, Phileleutherus, *A Defence of the British Constitution, against the Attacks of Civis, upon the Methodists and Dissenters etc.* (London, 1813), p. 22; and also Joseph Sutcliffe, *The Divine Mission of the People Called Methodists, to Revive and Spread Religion: Sermon . . . Macclesfield, May 27, 1813* (London: T. Blanshard [City Road], 1814), pp. 28-29, 30-31, 53-54.

. Halévy, in *England in 1815,* discussed these events of 1811 and 1812, observing that the government, at this time of national peril, had no wish to alienate and every reason to conciliate the Nonconformists.[44] (Indeed, it might be added that a surprising refrain of Methodist preaching during this period, in apparent contradiction to Methodism's usual appeals to divine right and passive obedience, was an invocation of the right of resistance if the protection of the Toleration Acts were withdrawn from the Connection.)[45] Halévy, however, did not tell his readers of the full terms of the debate between the friends and enemies of Methodism concerning Methodism and revolution. He appears to have understood the widespread iteration, in the generation after Wesley's death, of the Methodist claim of having blocked revolution as firsthand confirmation of the theory he had accepted from the hands of the French School, rather than as the party cry it obviously was. For whatever else may be said, the claim emerged as a party cry raised by the Methodists and their friends, not merely to counter a nearly century-old charge that the Methodists were fomenting revolution, but more specifically to beat back a renewal of such charges at a time when there were serious disturbances among the workingmen of the North, when the Established church was endeavoring to secure repressive legislation, and when the Dissenters and their hard-pressed Whig allies had every reason to wish to restrain a government whose taste for repression had already been amply revealed in the 1790s.

IV

Does such a view of the Halévy hypothesis – as having originated in a *parti pris* and a party cry, without much "hard" evidence to

44. Pp. 428-32.

45. See, for example, Henry Moore, *Fear God: Honour the King* (London: G. Paramore, 1794), pp. 20-23; Benjamin Rhodes, *A Discourse on Civil Government and Religious Liberty;* also *The Duties of Subjects to their Sovereign etc.* (Birmingham; J. Belcher, 1796), pp. 7-8; Thomas Roberts,

support it — mean that it ought to be abandoned? Decidedly not. The hypothesis, imaginatively qualified and extended, remains a highly stimulating one, worth further exploration. The program which Halévy drew up in 1906 has never been carried out; nor has there been any thoroughgoing attempt to deal with the subject.[46] (Indeed, it has been suggested that in an age of revisionist historiography the Halévy thesis has been regarded as passé merely because it has been assumed that a thesis over half a century old could not possibly continue to be useful![47]) The role played by Methodism in English history is certainly a complex one, and, as we have seen, contemporaries in both the eighteenth and nineteenth centuries found themselves divided on the central issue of whether Methodism favored or obstructed revolution — not unlike twentieth-century historians. Wearmouth, the Hammonds, and Thompson, for example, all found themselves with two views on the question: if the Hammonds saw Wilberforce as a villain and Evangelicalism as an opiate, they were nonetheless prepared to grant that Methodism had made many men "better rebels";[48] Wearmouth, while disputing the Halévy thesis in one book, took a rather different view in another;[49]

Christian Loyalty: A Sermon Delivered at the Methodist Chapel, King Street, Bristol . . . June 1, 1802 (Bristol: R. Edwards, 1802), pp. 5-6, 9, 27-30.

46. A vague attempt to realize the Halévy program may be seen in Maximin Piette, *La réaction wesleyenne dans l'évolution protestante;* translated as *John Wesley in the Evolution of Protestantism* (New York: Sheed and Ward, 1937); but, despite some nods in Halévy's direction, it fell short on all counts. See Halévy's review on M. Piette's *La réaction* in *Revue d'histoire écclésiastique* 23 (1927): 129-32. John Walsh, in his excellent essay "Origins of the Evangelical Revival," has observed that despite "the concentration of so much scholarship," continental as well as British, "only once have the origins of the Revival been treated in the round, in the brilliant but almost unknown essay by Halévy, written in 1906, which despite its shortcomings provided valuable methodological patterns that have never been followed up" (p. 132).

47. See Gertrude Himmelfarb, *Victorian Minds* (New York: Alfred A. Knopf, 1968), p. 299.

48. See Hammond, *Town Labourer*, p. 287.

49. See R.F. Wearmouth, *Methodism and the Working-Class Movements of England, 1800-1850* (London: Epworth Press, 1937); and *Methodism and the*

Thompson's explicit doubts concerning the thesis are balanced by an evident concurrent attraction to it.[50]

E. J. Hobsbawm, one of the most recent and thoroughgoing critics of the Methodist thesis, was similarly of two minds. On the one hand, Hobsbawm observed that Methodists, especially Primitive Methodists, were very much involved in radical activities in the early decades of the nineteenth century. It was "too easily assumed," he warned his readers, that industrial workers turned toward religious sects "*as an alternative* to revolution or radical politics"; he suggested that workers became Methodists or radicals for one and the same reasons.[51] On the other hand, Hobsbawm was to contrast French and British labor traditions in a way stongly suggestive of Halévy's approach of half a century earlier:

> Let us take a pair of extreme examples. In 1855 the slate-quarrymen of Trelaze, discontented with their economic conditions, decided to take action: they marched on Angers and proclaimed an insurrectionary Commune, presumably with the memory of the Commune of 1792 in their minds. Nine years later the coalminers of Ebbw Vale were equally agitated. The lodges from the valley villages marched on to the mountains, headed by bands. Speeches were made, tea provided by the Ebbw Vale lodge at 6d. a head and the meeting ended with the singing of the Doxology. Both Welsh miners and Breton quarry-men were engaged in rather similar economic agitations. Clearly they differed, because the histories of their respective countries had differed. The stock of past experience, upon which they drew in learning how to organize, what to organize

Common People of the Eighteenth Century.

50. Thompson's doubts are set forth on p. 45 of *The Making of the English Working Class.* His brilliant chapter "The Transforming Power of the Cross," however, may be regarded as confirming the thesis; see also p. 42. A further discussion of some of the complexities of Thompson's position on the Halévy thesis may be found in his postscript to the paperback edition (London: Penguin Books, 1968), pp. 917-23.

51. "Methodism and the Threat of Revolution in Britain," pp. 31-32. Hobsbawm takes much the same view in *Primitive Rebels* (New York: W.W. Norton, 1965), pp. 128-32, 145, and passim.

for, where to pick their cadre of leaders, and the ideology of those leaders embodied, in part at least, specific French and British elements: broadly speaking we may say, in the former case, of the revolutionary, in the latter of the radical-nonconformist traditions.[52]

Halévy, whose view of English history was shaped by his understanding of French development, found the answer to this difference in labor traditions, at least on the English side, in Methodism. In a letter to his mother written from London on 18 July 1905, when he was doing his research on eighteenth-century Methodism, Halévy described a visit on a Sunday evening to an open-air Methodist meeting in the City of London, to which he had been escorted by a young Methodist. Halévy, much moved, watched the minister, "the methodist pope of the neighborhood," followed by a great crowd which had been attracted by the sound of trumpets and trombones, leading the throng into a meeting-room of the Wesleyan Mission Hall, where a service, "extraordinary, mystic, benign, exalted, such as I had never previously seen," then took place. After a short period of prayers and hymn singing, the preacher, as Halévy observed, began his sermon:

Not a word about hell, not a word about death. But: "You are not alone. You are never alone. Jesus is with you, Jesus is near you, Jesus has put His hand on your shoulder." And, repeated several times, a phrase of a spiritual mesmerist: "Believe me, whatever you may think, whatever you may do, Jesus is here. You could not leave here in the same spirit in which you have come. You are helpless to change this. It is a fact. You could not leave here in the same spirit in which you have come." His finger is lifted, he leans over toward the five-hundred listeners present, he speaks very softly. He then asks that all rise to sing the third, the next to last stanza, of the hymn. Then, before coming to the fourth and last stanza, he asks those who have had that evening, for the first time or in an especially intense fashion, the sentiment of the presence of Jesus, not to be held back by any feeling of false modesty, but to rise to speak of it.

52. "Labour Traditions," in *Labouring Men*, pp. 371-72.

"What a strange people," Halévy concluded. "One can understand why, when they began to preach in the eighteenth century, they were regarded as a species of Jesuits," with "a smile, steadily and systematically, on their lips," intoning " 'See how good we are! See how we love each other! See how happy we are!' "

"I am getting to know England extremely well by studying the Methodists," Halévy wrote in beginning the above description of the Methodist service.[53] "Even today," he was to write in his 1906 articles, "whenever a Methodist preacher brings a popular audience together at a street corner to read the Bible, sing hymns, and pray in common, whenever he induces a 'revival' of mysticism and religious exaltation," it is "the great movement of 1739" which "is being repeated." In this way, "a force capable of expending itself in displays of violence or in popular upheavals, assumes, under the influence of a century and a half of Methodism, the form least capable of unsettling a social order." With the counterexample of France and of French history before him, he acknowledged, in a letter to Bouglé on 14 September 1905, that he was becoming an Anglophile. It was England which for many centuries had given Europe lessons in politics. By studying the history of England, Halévy concluded, he had lost his (French) fondness for "the beauty of revolutions." "What good was the enthusiasm of Jaurès," he asked, "if it was going to be overrun by the fanaticism of Hervé?"[54]

Halévy, then, was asking a question of prime importance, and he believed, on the basis of his study, his experience, and his historian's intuition, confirmed by the intuition and experience of leading French and English scholars in the past and by the views of many

53. Unpublished letter to Mme. Ludovic Halévy, London, 18 July 1905, made available to me by Dr. H. Noufflard Guy-Loé.

54. Unpublished letter to C. Bouglé, Sucy, 14 September 1905, made available to me by Dr. H. Noufflard Guy-Loé. See, in addition, a later letter to Bouglé, in 1908: "Si la Révolution n'avait eu ni les massacres de septembre, ni les noyades de Nantes, ni les guillotinades de Paris, et si par une suite peut-être nécessaire, elle avait fini par un Washington au lieu de finir par Bonaparte, je l'aimerais davantage." Alain, *Correspondance*, p.334.

insightful contemporaries of the Methodists during their early decades of growth, that he had found the answer in the influence of Methodism. In his articles for the *Revue de Paris* Halévy placed the essentials of the Methodist hypothesis in a context and imparted to them refinements which make them especially interesting to historians and social scientists today, and their translation will, I hope, enable English-speaking scholars to see the hypothesis in new, more powerful, and more dynamic terms than has heretofore been possible. As for the problem in its most simplistic form — did Methodism act as an obstacle to revolution? — a fully satisfactory solution is not to be expected. One friend of Methodism, writing in 1815, while making the usual claim that "the loyalty and patriotism of the Methodists is now well-known, both to the government itself and to the nation in general," concluded that the ultimate "usefulness" of the Methodists "in preventing the spread of French principles both political and religious, is only fully known to God."[55] It would be difficult for a responsible historian to fault this judgment.

55. Valentine Ward, *A Brief Statement of Facts, Designed for the Information of those Who from Good Motives Enquire "What are these Methodists?"* (Leeds: James Nichols, 1815), p. 82.

The Birth of Methodism
in England

I

The English are a nation of Puritans, and Puritanism is Protestantism taken in all the strictness of the dogma which constitutes its theological core — adherence to the doctrine of "justification by faith" originally propounded by Saint Paul. What is necessary for salvation, according to Saint Paul, and according to Luther and to Calvin as well, is not the performance of particular acts, nor the practice of specific rituals, nor anything which can subject us to the control of any group, church, or external authority; it is the immediate and mysterious relationship of the individual soul with the Deity.

This doctrine gives rise to the principle of tolerance which, when all is said and done, is an inseparable part of the Protestant spirit. Indeed, how can one not have a kind of superstitious awe for the human personality when the individual is regarded as an impenetrable temple in whose bosom God chooses to work the miracle of grace? And the doctrine also gives rise to that distrust both of ritualistic ceremonies, which require a clergy as intermediary between the faithful and God, and of the symbols by which the Catholic imagination strives to bring God closer to the perceptible world. Protestantism is a cold and austere faith, which can reach the sublime but in no way aspires to beauty. Its goal seems to be to convince the believer of the impossibility of man's ever comprehending the Deity in all his terrifying omnipotence. Protestantism is not a weakened Catholicism, it is a different kind of Christianity: one would be tempted to call it an altogether different religion. Catholicism is almost as far removed from Protestantism as Christianity is from

33

Mohammedanism. The Puritans can, in good part, be seen as the Muslims of the north — solemn, silent, proud, fearless, much like the Muslims of Africa.

Neither the advance of the commercial spirit and industrial civilization nor the development of the scientific spirit and critical rationalism, nor the prestige and pomp of Anglo-Catholic ritualism have been able to make England any less a nation of Puritans, even today. Across the Channel, religious awareness has not evolved as it has in the nations of continental Europe. In the Latin countries, traditional Catholicism and systematic irreligion are the opponents which face each other; in Protestant Germany, where the importance of sects is infinitely less than in England, Lutheranism with state support appears either as the national religion — the cult of the fatherland and the emperor — or as a spiritual philosophy for the use of university professors. We see nothing like this in England. Why is there such a difference?

England has not always been regarded as a nation of Puritans. She had an entirely different reputation in the years following the revolution of 1688, when the modern history of the kingdom really began.

The English Whigs, who at that time effected a change in dynasties, thus assuring themselves of power for many years, were aristocrats, but aristocrats who claimed the support of the middle class and the common people: they were dedicated revolutionaries who pulled off the rather extraordinary feat of setting up the rights of revolution, of regicide, and of irreligion as principles of government in the midst of the "century of Louis XIV." They installed at the head of the Anglican clergy latitudinarian bishops, who were equally hostile to Puritan "enthusiasm" and Catholic "superstition," and whose preaching amounted to instruction in natural religion and social ethics.

At the same time, the ministers of the Nonconformist sects, which had come into being at the time of the civil and religious wars and had until then been centers of Illuminism, seemed to relax their Calvinist intransigence. Content at having contributed to the overthrow of the catholicizing Stuart dynasty and having secured legal toleration for the practice of their faith, they turned their backs on fanaticism and became, in matters of doctrine, open-minded and rationalist.

Finally, there arose, outside the religious sects, a party of philosophers whose system consisted entirely in a denial of Christianity. They disputed the historical arguments in support of the Christian revelation supposedly found in the Bible. They leveled accusations of chicanery at priestly miracle makers and the authors of tracts claiming divine inspiration. They affirmed the uselessness of revelation and the timelessness of natural religion and morality, awaiting the day when they would pass from Deism to a systematic atheism. Before the France of Voltaire, England had its freethinkers. Before the Germany of Kant, she had her critical philosophers. Contemporaries appraising the British national consciousness formed their judgment on the basis of the philosophic outlook of those who boasted that they had shaped that consciousness. England therefore appeared to be the pale of irreligion par excellence. She was the inspirer of all European irreligion. This was the time when Voltaire and Montesquieu, crossing the Channel, discovered with delight a land where incredulity was in good taste, and where it was generally accepted that one could be both a good citizen and a bad Christian.

But after fifty years (1688-1738) of professing religious skepticism England had her Puritan revival, and the date can be established firmly: it was in 1739 that the crisis occurred. The revival made steady progress until the end of the eighteenth century, and it left indelible marks upon the consciousness of the English people. To study this revival and to know its causes would be to answer, at least in part, the question we have asked ourselves: Why has modern England remained a Puritan nation?

Historians often explain the revival of 1739 in a way that is much too simple to be entirely satisfactory. They attribute it to the influence of a few individuals endowed with a genius for leadership and organization, men sufficiently fervent, eloquent, and energetic to alter, in lasting fashion, the consciousness of an entire nation.

Toward 1730, several Oxford students, nearly all of them candidates for ecclesiastical ordination, formed a small religious society. They prayed together and attended the sick and prisoners.

They astonished and shocked the city by their exalted piety. A few of them were to be remembered by history: Hervey, the future man of letters, the tedious, moralizing, and mannered author of *Meditations among the Tombs;* George Whitefield, a man of the people, the son of a Gloucester stableman, who by firmness of resolution and his own efforts had got to Oxford — an eloquent, passionate, violent man whose emotional life was tormented by strange crises. Foremost among them were Charles and John Wesley, the two sons of an Anglican minister: Charles, sweet, sentimental, poetic, and mild; and John, a born leader who was the spiritual chieftain of this band. They were covered with ridicule; sobriquets were heaped upon them. They were called "the Club of Saints"; they were also dubbed "the Methodists" because of the rigorously "methodical" and regulated character of their ascetic practices. The name struck home, and for some time there was much talk of the "Oxford Methodists." Then, having concluded their studies, they dispersed. Some of them went off to evangelize, with modest success, the Georgia colonists and the American Indians. And for some years they were forgotten.

Toward the end of 1738, the leading members of this group found themselves reunited, not at Oxford, but in London; and once more they attracted public attention. John Wesley, Charles Wesley, and George Whitefield preached from church pulpits the dogma of justification by faith, and crowds flocked in to hear them. By the fiery, passionate nature of their eloquence, by the intransigence of their theology, by the very success they enjoyed — a success that aroused envy — they angered the incumbents of the parishes in which they requested permission to preach. They were denounced to the ecclesiastical authorities, and the churches were closed to them. So they preached at the church doors, in the streets, in the open fields. The revival of 1739 had begun.

Immense crowds gathered about the Methodist preachers: one thousand, ten thousand, fifty thousand, up to eighty thousand listeners at one time. John Wesley and George Whitefield revolutionized religious rhetoric. Rather than imitate the fashionable sermonizers by reciting well-prepared addresses of a polished and pedantic character, they improvised their sermons and aimed at generating violent emotions in their listeners, at filling them with terror of hell, or, more precisely, with dread of sin, which is the true hell. Their great talent (which, they prided themselves, was much more than a mere clever stratagem) was to produce, in the breasts of those who heard them, a crisis of despair followed by a sudden relaxation and a mood of blissful peace. They performed genuine wonders. They inspired sudden fits of fainting, convulsions. In the semibarbaric provinces, which no one had thought of either civilizing or Christianizing since the Reformation, in the industrial regions in which an ever-denser population, lacking schools and churches, was crowding, thousands were "converted" by their sermons.

They had hoped that the Methodist "society" would remain a kind of Anglican order of brother-preachers or, more exactly, a kind of lay third order, working side by side with the clergy to "revivify" the established church. Circumstances determined that they would become the founders of a new sect, which would be the most powerfully organized, the richest, and the largest of all the Protestant denominations. And their range of activity extended beyond that of their own sect.

They reanimated, as a side effect of their influence, the other Dissenting sects, which were seemingly dying of old age; these were instilled with new youth. They regenerated the Church of England at the very moment when that church was driving them from her bosom; the most zealous of the clergy of the established church imitated their oratorical method and adopted their fundamental doctrine. They even had an effect upon freethinkers, who subsequently refrained from criticizing Christian doctrine in order to devote themselves to political economy and philanthropy. Utilitarians and evangelicals agreed to work together for commercial freedom, the abolition of slavery, and the reform of criminal law and prison organization. Never, it might be said, has the influence of two or three individuals appeared as deep and as undeniable: is it possible to conceive of Methodism without John Wesley and Whitefield? Yet, how can we say that a movement which has absorbed so many millions of men would not have come to pass if two clergymen, John Wesley and George Whitefield, had not lived?

We must first set down in its true proportions the religious revolution of 1739 from which Methodism sprang, a revolution which had been prompted by the preaching of Wesley and Whitefield. These two preachers wanted to reawaken or to revive, in a form more suitable to contemporary circumstances, the old Puritan faith which had triumphed a century earlier at the time of Cromwell's republic. But is it possible that this Puritanism, which exerted so much influence on the nation for a century, had undergone such a sharp decline as not to leave deep marks on the popular consciousness? Historians have endeavored to dramatize the revival: beforehand, absolute irreligion and immorality; afterward, through the preaching of Wesley and Whitefield, a sudden mood of universal exaltation. But the truth is less simple.

It was without doubt customary, at the beginning of the eighteenth century, to contrast France, the country of administrative and religious despotism, with England, a "republic," in some ways anticlerical, where unlimited freedom of opinion was regarded as the foundation of the national constitution. But such a view, in the last analysis, bears only upon the most aristocratic and superficial part of each nation. Contemporary witnesses, properly understood, suggest how much latent religious sentiment the English temperament still harbored.

We are told that France at that time was a clerical nation, England an irreligious one. But we are also told that the Frenchman was gay, light-hearted, expansive, and frivolous, and that the Englishman was grave, reserved, silent, and melancholy: spleen, vapors, all the forms of *melancholia* were regarded as being preeminently "the English Malady." Was this apparently congenital melancholy the effect, as certain physicians of the time asserted, of an oppressive and wet climate and of the oversedentary life that was led in large and overpopulated cities? Was it not also the effect of the Puritan indoctrination, fanatic and grimly zealous, to which the English people had submitted during the seventeenth century? Whatever the causes of this *melancholia* may have been, it had certain effects. When it did not lead to suicide (the growing number of suicides was constantly being deplored by English writers of the eighteenth century), it lent itself to religious meditation and turned the soul of its victim to prayer and asceticism.

Open the then well-known tome, by Dr. Cheyne on "the English Malady," and read his description of the black infirmity with which he struggled all his life.[1] Then read the little work in which John Cennick, George Whitefield's lieutenant, one of the first converts to Methodism, set forth the emotional distresses that beset him until the day of his conversion.[2] Both men are speaking of the same malady, and the physician prescribes a medication that is a kind of religious asceticism. The temperament of the freethinker is quite different: in order to call into doubt the authenticity of a book so sacred that it fills the human race with awe, in order to blaspheme the gods, souls less accessible to worry and doubt are required; more carefree and, if you like, more frivolous temperaments are needed.

It is of course true that the nonbelievers in England had been enjoying the most complete liberty of opinion since 1688; but who can tell whether, in this very tolerance, which the English allowed even their most irreligious fellow citizens to benefit from, there was not hidden a kind of religiosity? That a man constituted as I am, and for whom the truth should be the same as it is for me, may have an entirely different opinion, that his consciousness should be in some respects transparent and in others impenetrable to my own — there is the incomprehensible mystery. If religious sentiment, in its essence, is reverence for the incomprehensible, could this not be seen as the mystic foundation of English liberalism? Liberalism, thus defined, would imply both the conviction that our reason meets with insurmountable barriers in its course, and reverence for, or, if

1. *The English Malady or a Treatise of Nervous Diseases of all Kinds, as Spleen, Vapours, Lowness of Spirits, Hypochondriacal and Hysterical Distempers, etc., with the Author's own case at large,* by George Cheyne, fellow of the College of Physicians at Edinburgh. London, 1735.

2. *The Life of Mr. J. Cennick, with an Account of the Trials and Temptations which he endured till it pleased our Saviour to show him his Love, and send him into his Vineyard.* Written by Himself, for their Sakes who follow the Lamb. 2d ed., Bristol, 1745.

you like, awe of, those things in nature which escape our intelligence. To this outlook, so characteristic of the English in modern times, French rationalism was singularly unsusceptible.

A century of Cartesian education had already convinced the French of 1740 that nothing in the universe could be said to be incomprehensible in the final analysis; that it was not possible to set limits to the advance of reason. France was the more "clerical" of the two great nations. But even this apparent clericalism may have been hiding more fundamental incredulity than did the liberal regime of which England could boast. In 1737, a short time before Wesley became an apostle in England, and Voltaire a demigod in France, a London journalist was sufficiently perceptive to criticize the prevailing opinion: "Do not be deceived on this point," he wrote; "nature has endowed the French with sharp, penetrating minds. Were they free to give their genius full play, no people on earth would push their conclusions further. The English delude themselves when they think they reason more soundly: their sole advantage is that they permit themselves to be guided by their imagination, and do not always feel obliged to draw conclusions based on false premises."[3]

But while it may be demonstrated that the English were melancholy, that a melancholy people are a religious people, and that, perhaps, in the very liberalism that they evidenced in their attitude toward irreligion, they were still unconsciously following religious inspiration, it does not remain less true that liberal institutions made possible the propagation of irreligious ideas, and that in the long run the progress of irreligion, by its gradual transformation of the national psyche, was able to make the English less melancholy at the same time that it was making them less theological. All contemporaries seem to agree in recognizing that the established church was daily becoming more discredited, and that the religious activities of the Dissenters were, during the same period, singularly sluggish. Historians have on the whole confirmed the judgment of contemporaries. On a point which seems to lend itself to so little dispute, in

3. *Fog's Weekly Journal,* 12 March 1737.

what measure ought we contradict once again the evidence of both contemporaries and historians?

So far as the established church is concerned, it is usual to stress the spiritless rationalism of preachers at that time and the absence of zeal and culture among the country parsons. Historians have properly noted that the triumph of the Whig party, a party allied with all those in the nation who were hostile to the privileges of the Church of England, must necessarily have exerted a depressing influence on a church so strictly subordinated to state authority. However, let us not exaggerate the decline of the religious spirit in the Anglican church. Numerous associations were founded within the church, voluntarily and without state help, to battle vice and to enlighten the faithful; their very existence proves that the decline was not as deep or as general as people might claim.

There was the Society for the Promotion of Christian Knowledge, founded in 1696 for the purpose of founding Charity Schools (free primary schools); distributing Bibles, prayerbooks, and tracts; preaching in the workhouses, and giving aid to persecuted Protestants on the continent. In 1701, a second society, the Society for the Propagation of the Gospel in Foreign Parts, formed from the first, strove to set up Anglican missions on the model of Catholic missions. There also were Societies for the Reformation of Manners (the first dates from 1688), peculiar voluntary associations founded to institute supervision of morals in the large towns, in London, Bristol, Canterbury, Nottingham, and others. In London, thanks to a well-organized system of judicial assistance and official spying, members of the society were proud of having secured more than a thousand convictions for blasphemy, drunkenness, and Sabbath-breaking, more than a thousand convictions for assault or soliciting, and the closing of five hundred houses of prostitution. Finally, and still more symptomatic, there were the Religious Societies, formed in large numbers in London as well as in the provinces for the mutual edification of those who took part.[4]

4. See Chamberlayne, *State of England,* chap. 9, on these various societies.

Members of these societies pledged that they would solicit advice in all doubtful or difficult cases from the clergy of the established church, receive Holy Communion at least once a month, and take every opportunity to attend divine services; they endeavored to organize prayer meetings in the churches, to make certain that Communion was administered weekly, and to see to it that sermons were given every Sunday on the Sacrament of Holy Communion.

They visited the poor, the sick, the prisoners. They boasted of having converted Quakers and Enthusiasts to the necessity for being baptized and for submitting to church rites; they claimed to have kept many waverers from a descent into papism. The society of students that John Wesley and his friends formed at Oxford in 1729 was but one of these associations, and its program, which has been preserved for us by Wesley, is identical to those of the other Religious Societies. The only difference between the Oxford Methodists and the members of other local societies, was that the former were younger and consequently more courageous, more disposed to provoking public attention by the display of their asceticism.

After the two Wesleys and George Whitefield had left Oxford, the society vegetated; by 1735 it seems to have entirely disappeared. Are we to assume that the existence of the other Religious Societies was as fragile? This view is generally maintained; we are told that by the end of 1738, when the preaching of Methodism began, they were all in decline. These would have had to be the circumstances if we wished to depict Methodism as an absolutely new event, a veritable historical miracle. But the history of Methodist preaching itself, in 1738 and 1739, proves how poorly founded such a view is.

It was, indeed, upon the Religious Societies in London and in the provinces that the two Wesleys and Whitefield first launched their propaganda. They found these societies numerous and flourishing; they succeeded so well in penetrating them with their influence that it is often difficult to say whether, during the three years which preceded their break with the established church, when the Methodists speak of a society, they mean a new association that they formed to spread their doctrine or one of the earlier Religious

Societies that was now open, by the will of its members, to their new preaching.

In sum, the seeds of religious renovation had existed for a considerable time within the Anglican Church, and Methodism emerged from one of these seeds. However, the Methodism of 1739 that John Wesley preached in the public squares was different from the Oxford Methodism that ten years earlier had been the doctrine of Wesley and his friends at the university. The name persisted; the inspiration had been transformed. In the interval, John Wesley had himself been "converted," if not to a new religion, at least to a new way of understanding and of "experiencing" the Christian religion.

When this religious renovation was accomplished, the entire Anglican church as well as the Religious Societies broke with the former Oxford Methodists, who were now suspected of a lack of discipline and of heresy.

Why were the societies formed by the Anglican church at the beginning of the eighteenth century powerless to bring forth a revival themselves? Because the Protestant, or Puritan, impulse had failed them, and this was indispensable if they were to act upon the conscience of the nation.

No church without religion: this was the truth the Protestant loved to stress, and the most essential element in the Protestant conception of the Christian life was not the union of many consciences in a common faith; it was the direct union of the individual conscience with the Creator. No religion without a church, the Catholic replied, insisting that God permitted the individual, powerless by his own efforts, to lift himself up to Him, to become capable of faith, only if he allowed himself to be supported by the authority of a Church and the practice of a ritual.

The most zealous members of the Anglican church, when Wesley was studying at Oxford, were adherents of this Catholic point of view. They were High Churchmen, or, as we would say today, Anglo-Catholics. They emphasized the need for an ecclesiastical institution when they attempted, before the Puritan revival of 1739, to restore the national religion by other means. They defended the hierarchy in all matters. In politics they were filled with hostility and contempt for the usurping dynasty, for its ministers, and for the Whig party. John Wesley, at Oxford, was a Jacobite; one of the Oxford Methodists who refused to participate in the revival of 1739 was to compromise himself in the Pretender's attempt in 1745 to invade England at the head of his Scottish soldiery. In ecclesiastical matters they aimed at increasing the prestige and privileges of the clergy.

They were proud of having persuaded a number of Enthusiasts — intransigent Protestants who disputed the efficacy of rites and believed that inner conversion sufficed to make a Christian — of the error of their ways. Their ambition was to wage victorious battle against Roman Catholic propaganda, at the same time attenuating, as far as possible, the Protestant aspects of Anglican discipline and dogma. What was the the meaning of the nickname inflicted on the "Methodists" at Oxford, and taken up by them with pride? "Methodism," in the last analysis, is virtually synonymous with "Ritualism": the religious preoccupations of Wesley and his friends, in 1729, must have been very much like those that engaged Newman and the High Churchmen of his generation a century later at the same university. For the Oxford Methodists, as for the members of all the Religious Societies, it was a question of affirming that there was no sound piety without the "method" and "rites" prescribed by ecclesiastical tradition.

Here we may discover why the efforts made by the Anglican church before 1740 to touch the popular consciousness had failed. If John Wesley, having gone to Georgia as a missionary, returned, most miserably, some three years later, pursued by the hoots of those he had wished to enlighten and reform, it was probably, in large part, because of an unhappy love affair from which he had emerged very clumsily; but it was also because of the rigorous orthodoxy which this High Churchman, the son of a High Churchman and educated at Oxford, had attempted to impose upon a colonial population, deeply imbued with Protestant convictions. And it is for similar reasons that the Religious Societies had not been able to exert a profound influence in England. The members who composed them were moved by a sincere sense of religion; but they were Jacobites, and the country was Whig. They wanted to convert the nation to

High Church principles, but the English bourgeoisie remained stead-
fastly Protestant.

Where can this English Protestantism — which, as we have said,
persisted so tenaciously — be found if not in the dissenting sects that
preened themselves on having braved persecution for a century in
order to maintain the Protestant tradition? And what then becomes
of the theory, widely accepted by historians and thoroughly in line
with contemporary opinion, that the Dissenting sects had been in
decline ever since the revolution of 1688?[5]

The writings and sermons of the principal Dissenting ministers are
invoked in support of this theory. They were rationalists, proud of
their superior erudition and education, proud of their schools, the
Academies, which they had established almost everywhere, and
which were attended by young men of the highest society. They
were liberals, falling out with Calvinist theology, even inclined to
admit on occasion that, without ceasing to be a good Christian, one
could become semi-Arian, Arian, or even a Socinian, denying the
divinity of Jesus Christ.

Such attitudes and tendencies were not such as would promote
the conversion of nonbelievers and gain souls for the ranks of
Dissent. By 1730, the Dissenters were alarmed to see their ministers,
in growing numbers, deserting Nonconformity and joining the ranks
of the Anglican clergy. Disturbing symptoms, to be sure; but if this
was true of the ministers, was it of all the faithful?

One must not judge a church, especially a free church, by its
clergy alone. The decline of Dissent at the beginning of the eighteenth century, seems to have been caused principally by the indif-

5. See *An Enquiry into the causes of the Decay of the Dissenting Interest,
in a letter to a dissenting minister, 1729. Free Thoughts on the most probable
means of reviving the dissenting interest, occasioned by the late enquiry, into
the causes of its decay.* Addressed to the author of that enquiry, by Philip
Doddridge, 1729. See also Some (David), *Two Sermons: the first on the
methods to be taken by ministers for the revival of religion, and the other
occasioned by the death of Rev Thomas Sounders of Kettering,* 2d ed., 1754
(the first sermon was delivered in 1729.)

ference of the ministers rather than the apathy of the flocks. Despite the pastors, the mass of English Nonconformists remained attached to the old Protestant doctrine of justification by faith and to all the religious emotions which are inseparable parts of that doctrine.

In order to determine the true state of mind of the Dissenters on the eve of the Methodist movement, we would have to study the local histories of the smallest congregations and search out the real conflict behind the quarrels which constantly divided them among themselves. The Independents claimed the absolute autonomy of each congregation and the absolute subordination of the pastors to the faithful. But English law compelled them to delegate chapel property to trustees, usually the richest men in the congregation: and it often happened that the majority of the poor members were in conflict with the trustees when the latter, setting themselves up as proprietors of the place of worship, sought to impose an unpopular pastor upon them.

Occasionally the morals of the minister were denounced. At other times, the dispute concerned matters of ritual: the Baptists were sharply divided on the question of whether it was permissible to admit to Communion those who had not been baptized as adults and by immersion, as prescribed by the principle of their sect. Or again, it might be dogma itself that was at issue. Arians in growing numbers were asking if the placing of the Father and the Son on the same level in the Holy Trinity, did not contradict the dogma of divine Unity. Liberal Arminians charged the advocates of predestination that their doctrine led to the immoral thesis of antinomianism — the view that the moral law was abolished for the Elect of the Lord. In turn, orthodox Calvinists charged the advocates of human free will with all kinds of heresies, and lumped them, with almost the same feelings of revulsion, together with freethinkers, and Deists.

Ministers usually decried these disputes, to their mind both useless and troublesome. Above all, they dreaded the fanaticism of the orthodox. They attempted to withdraw from the quarrels. They devoted themselves in their sermons to the preaching of tolerance and the discrediting of religious enthusiasm. Usually they failed, a schism occurred in the congregation, and the pastor, suspected of heresy or indifference, was abandoned by half of his flock. But are such schisms within Dissenting churches symptoms or causes of weakness? A free church has not the same need for unity as a state church: to divide and subdivide continuously is perhaps the normal law of its development. The divisions and quarrels were, in reality, proof of the passion with which the Dissenters continued to defend the beliefs for which their fathers had fought and suffered. It often happened that the minister, at the end of his patience, deserted Dissent. Why did this occur? It was simply because, exhausted by the religious fervor of the faithful, he sought the peace of an official, hierarchical church, where the pastor at least did not have to submit to the theological demands of his sheep.

Everywhere in the history of Nonconformity during that period we see signs of this spiritual divorce between ministers and their congregations. A minister in Exeter, James Pierce, for example, was charged with heresy by the laity of the area and, when they had obtained his condemnation by the ministers, driven from town to town by congregations to which he came to offer himself as pastor.[6] Then there was Calamy, one of the great Dissenters, who, arriving in a small town and invited by his host to preach at his house that evening, suddenly saw that he was the victim of a trap: the laity were unhappy with the local minister, whom Calamy knew and

6. On this curious incident, which produced a considerable uproar and provoked a kind of schism within English Dissent, see, besides such general works as Bogue and Bennet, *History of the Dissenters,* and Ivimey, *History of the Baptists,* all the pamphlets which the affair produced at a time when religious fervor was supposedly extinguished, principally: *A True Account of what was Transacted in the Assembly of the United Ministers of Devon and Cornwall, Met at Exon the 5th and 6th of May 1719,* by those Ministers who signed the first Article of the Church of England, etc. Exeter, 1719; *A Plain and Faithful Narrative of the Differences Among the Dissenters, at Exeter, Relating to the Doctrine of the Ever Blessed Trinity, so far as gave Concern to some London Ministers,* London, 1719; *The Anatomy of the Heretical Synod of Dissenters at Salters Hall . . . ,* by the Author of Scourge. In a letter to a Country Friend, London, 1719; *The Western Inquisition, or a Relation of the Controversy which has been lately among the Dissenters in the West of England,* by James Pierce, London, 1720.

valued, but whom they found not sufficiently orthodox for their tastes; they hoped to convince Calamy to set up a rival chapel; terrified, deafened by their pleas and cries, he fled, abandoning his defense of his colleague against the charges heaped upon him.[7] There was also the case of Doddridge, another great Dissenter, who was invited to become minister at Northampton, and for a long time could not make up his mind. Accustomed to more polished congregations, he was frightened off by the pervasive atmosphere of Calvinist fanaticism.[8]

Of the three main Dissenting denominations, Presbyterianism was the one in which Socinianism and all forms of rationalism made the greatest advances, precisely because its constitution was the least democratic and its ministry the least subjected to lay control. When the Methodists started to preach through the breadth of England, they were well received by the great majority of Dissenters. Was not the religion they preached a revival of Puritanism? But they ran up against the distrust and hatred of the ministers, too enlightened and reasonable to enjoy the doctrine and method of the Awakening.[9] And that is why those ministers were not themselves capable of bringing forth an Awakening; and why the Awakening could not come from the Dissenting churches.

7. Calamy, *Account of his own life,* p. 301 ff.

8. Doddridge, *Correspondence and Diary,* letter to Dr. Wright, 8 November 1729. Doddridge appears to have been partially converted to the need for a Puritan revival by the very atmosphere in which he found himself situated. In his *Free Thoughts,* he insists on the need to be "an evangelical, an experimental, a plain & an affectionate preacher" in order to satisfy the Dissenting public; and he explains very well that the cause of the decay of Dissent lies in the rationalism of the ministers, who do not satisfy the spiritual needs of their congregations. Subsequently he will unleash the anger of all his colleagues against himself by entering into friendly relations with Whitefield, and by allowing the latter to preach from his pulpit (See *Correspondence,* from 27 June 1743 onward).

9. The very different attitude of the Dissenting ministers and the laymen toward the revival is curiously revealed in *A brief Account of the late Persecution and Barbarous Usage of the Methodists at Exeter, wherein the characters of the Rioters, their Aiders and Abettors, are fully described . . . ,* by an impartial Hand. Exon, 1745.

Such, in the last analysis, was the religious state of England on the eve of the Methodist movement. The clergy of the established church had much more zeal and fervor than is ordinarily granted, but the most fervent of these clergymen were also the most dedicated to High Church principles. If these priests wished to re-Christianize the nation, they first had to recognize the impossibility of converting England to their class prejudices; they themselves had first to return to the true Protestant faith. For Protestant passions persisted in the mass of the nation: the public was seized with violent emotion whenever a journalist or pamphleteer, as in 1737, drew its attention to the real or supposed advance of papist propaganda. Panic would break out. Freethinkers and good Christians alike demanded a more rigorous application of the laws against the Catholics; Anglican clergymen and Dissenting ministers competed in the vituperation with which they denounced Rome and its religious policy. The Dissenting ministers should have been able to assume the leadership of this Protestant opinion; they were its chosen chiefs. But betraying the confidence of their followers, they preached a doctrine more and more like Deism, a morality more and more like that of Aristotle or Cicero, instead of Christianity according to Saint Paul. To produce such a revival of faith, what was needed was a combination of the ecclesiastical zeal of certain of the clergy, and the Protestant piety of the mass of the faithful. Was Methodism anything but this?

Consider Methodist dogmatics: they are a mixture of the two elements we have just noted. The Methodists begin by stressing that preeminently Protestant doctrine, justification by faith. To be saved, it is not sufficient that the mind be convinced that there is a God and that man has sinned and that God has descended onto earth to redeem him. What we have known since the resurrection of Christ, demons have known for a much longer time. But are the demons Christian? Are they saved? To be saved, we need the immediate certainty of salvation, by the miracle of faith which does not merely promise us the joys of paradise for a later time if we fulfill certain conditions, but which frees us from sin and its terrors immediately, and on this earth. This faith is the free gift of God. It is vain to hope that by the exercise of our free will we might strive to deserve it. From all eternity, God, in the plenitude of his omnipotence, has willed that some be saved and others, in much greater numbers, be damned.

Such had always been the view of the best Calvinist logicians; such was still the view of some among the first Methodists, and of George Whitefield in particular. Wesley, however, rebelled against this logic. He had been raised in the beliefs of the High Church; and the High Church had always been Arminian, not Calvinist. He declared that one might maintain the dogma of justification by faith, along with Saint Paul, and still have room for the doctrine of Saint James, for the dogma of justification by works and for the theory of free will. This eclecticism, which logic may call inadmissible, gave novelty and force to the Puritanism revived by Wesley. The doctrine of justification by faith remained an inexhaustible source of religious emotion for the Protestant conscience. Wesley kept it. The dogma of predestination implied a series of theological enormities to which modern rationalism could not accommodate itself, and of moral atrocities whose tragic quality the modern conscience could not endure. It was a stroke of luck for the Methodist movement that John Wesley, by dint of the prejudices of his early education, felt an invincible repugnance for predestination.

Also consider the discipline and ecclesiastical organization of Methodism: there we find the same eclecticism, the same concili- ation of contrary principles. Methodism is certainly a Protestant Church; from the beginning, laymen had the right to preach. We would not, however, suggest that in the Methodist Church, by Luther's formula, "every man is a priest." John Wesley remained throughout his life an Anglican clergyman and, moreover, a clergy- man instinctively attached to certain High Church principles. For a long time, he refused his lay preachers the right to administer the sacraments. Under the pressure of circumstances and to keep them from deserting his societies, he ended by yielding this right to some of those who assisted him; but it was to those only upon whom, by the laying on of hands, he believed he was conferring the mystic powers that he had received at his own ordination.

A very sharp distinction has persisted, among Methodists, between these ministers and the mass of laymen, a distinction much sharper than that which exists in the other Nonconformist churches. Methodist ministers are not regarded as men chosen by their congregations. Ordained, then sent to their posts by the assembly of pastors in conference, they must be replaced every three years so as not to be subjected too strictly to the influence of those whose spiritual guidance has been delegated to them. According to the ecclesiastical spirit of Wesleyanism, they belong to their order more than to their congregation; since the death of Wesley, the entire history of the Methodist Church in England has consisted of the efforts of the pastors to diminish as much as possible the authority over the church exercised by the lay faithful.

Methodism is the High Church of Nonconformity. It is a Nonconformist sect established by Anglican clergymen who wished to remain faithful to the Church of England. From this stemmed the success of Methodism at a time when England was weary of the Christian republicanism of the seventeenth century and when a new kind of republicanism had not yet arisen elsewhere in Europe to wage war on the very concept of religion.

In Wesleyan organization, the hierarchical and the egalitarian principles were combined in equal portions. A moderately conservative Protestantism was substituted for the revolutionary Protestantism of the seventeenth century. In 1649, the English Puritans had beheaded a king. It is generally agreed that the influence of Methodism contributed a great deal, during the last several years of the eighteenth century, to preventing the French Revolution from having an English counterpart.

The evangelical revival of 1739, as we have seen, was not a completely new initiative, a phenomenon *ex nihilo:* it consisted of well-defined, preexisting elements in a new combination. But so long as these elements remained separated, so long as the misunderstanding that we have endeavored to describe and explain persisted in the religious consciousness of England, it was inevitable that rationalism make a gradual but continuous advance. To stop or to slow down this advance, to produce this new combination of forces, an accident proved necessary.

This accident was not only the existence of John Wesley and Whitefield, and their joining together. Neither one of them considered evangelizing England when they left Oxford. For Methodism to be born, their mission had first to be revealed to them. Neither had yet discovered that dogma the preaching of which was to become the core of Methodism: they had first to be converted, so to speak, to Protestantism. This conversion took place in 1738 and in 1739. What were the chance circumstances which brought it about? To this we must now turn close attention if we wish to understand the causes of the Methodist revival.

II

England, since it was the heart of European Protestantism, had become a place of exile to which the most zealous French and German Protestants, those who preferred expatriation and ruin to apostasy, emigrated. Similarly, in our day, democrats or revolutionaries, the political outlaws of the continent, come to London to find refuge. But the religious refugees of the eighteenth century were much more numerous, and more influential. If, because of a regime of universal tolerance, the old Puritan exaltation sometimes tended to be stilled, it was awakened as a result of these foreign influences. This is what happened in 1739. "That mixture of Skepticism and Enthusiasm which disturbs us for the present," the correspondent of one journal wrote, "we derive from the German and French Refugees."[10]

French Huguenots had already arrived in England in the sixteenth century, after the Saint Bartholomew's Eve massacre. They came in great numbers after the revocation of the Edict of Nantes. They filled entire neighborhoods in England, Scotland, and Ireland. In London, to minister to their spiritual needs, they maintained up to thirty-five Huguenot churches. Among these exiles were shrewd

10. Boyer, *Political State of England,* July 1739.

manufacturers and fine artisans, men who made their fortune in their new fatherland; mystics and eccentrics were also among them. In 1707, three fugitives from the Cévennes astonished London with scenes of illuminism, prophecy, and hysteria. Solemnly repudiated by the ministers of the Huguenot churches, condemned by the courts, they nevertheless succeeded in establishing a small church, thanks to the financial and moral support of a rich and credulous burgher. It was called, after their benefactor, Lacy's Congregation, or, by its better known name, the Church of the "French Prophets."[11]

The French Prophets exorcised those possessed by demons, remitted sins, claimed to be able to revive the dead. Did they exert an influence on a burgeoning Methodism? It has been said that Whitefield borrowed the title for one of his earlier writings from John Lacy.[12] But we are not sure about this, and we are sure, on the other hand, that John Wesley, having attended the services of the French Prophets, emerged with an even stronger bias against the hysterical seizures which were also a feature of his own societies. The contagious influence of the preaching of the Prophets of the Cévennes upon the London public is nonetheless a significant fact; it helps us better to understand the influence exerted by other refugees upon the spirit of John Wesley and his group.

Many thousands of Germans arrived from the Palatinate in 1709; in 1732, after the Salzburg persecutions, there was a new flood of

11. For the history of this sect, see *The Honest Quaker, or, the Forgeries and Impostures of the Pretended French Prophets and their abettors expos'd, in a letter from a Quaker to his Friend, giving an Account of a Sham-Miracle perform'd by John L − y esq. on the body of Elizabeth Gray, on the 17th of August last,* London, 1707. *A Caveat against New Prophets, in two Sermons at the Merchants' Lecture in Salters Hall, on Jan. the 6th and Jan. the 20th. 1707-8,* by Edmond Calamy, London, 1708. *The History of Modern Enthusiasm, from the Reformation to the present Times,* by Theophilus Evans, London, 1752 (pp. 57-67).

12. Evans, *History of Modern Enthusiasm,* p. 70: "Whether it was in imitation of John Lacy, Esq. who had published a Pamphlet of *God's Dealings with him . . . ,* I know not, but, in fact, he wrote also, when very young, two Pamphlets, entitled *God's Dealings with George Whitefield.*"

immigrants. Then came members of a small mystical church, established in the Middle Ages, whose adherents regarded it as the oldest of all the Protestant churches: the Moravian Brethren. Persecuted at home, they had at first found a refuge in Saxony at Herrnhut, on the lands of Count Zinzendorf, a strange personage, deeply pious, not without a kind of genius, but authoritarian, violent, quackish, whose ambition was to regenerate the society of the Brethren and to have it play a new role in the history of Christianity.[13]

Instead of a missionizing church seeking to make spiritual conquests at the expense of others, he dreamed of a small church of the initiated, which would seek to infiltrate all the Protestant churches and to instill a new spirit. A disciple of Spener and the German Pietists, Zinzendorf declared war on the prevailing Deism and endeavored to restore the belief in the only God with whom our religion and morality could be concerned, not merely a God endowed with physical attributes, the creator of matter and of the eternal laws which govern matter, but a God who can and who wants to save us, the redeeming God, the God incarnate, Jesus Christ. He set himself up as protector of all the persecuted Protestants on the Continent. Of noble family and a German, assured of support at the court of George II, he secured facilities for the settling of German refugees in the new English colony of Georgia. Moravian missionaries departed to assist the colonists and to spread the gospel among the Redskins. He had restored the Moravian episcopacy: to give greater weight to the new title, he sought and secured from the Archbishop of Canterbury recognition of its validity by the Church of England. Finally, he got in touch with the sincerely religious men of the Church of England, with the members of the Religious Societies, in order to convert them to the inner and "experimental" Christianity, to the dogma of justification by faith. A valuable source of knowl-

13. On the Moravian Brethren and their English activities, see Wesley's *Journals,* and *Memoirs of James Hutton,* by D. Benham (London, 1856), and a short monograph: *Die Anfänge der Brüderkirche in England, Ein Kapitel vom geistigen Austausch Deutschlands und Englands,* by G.-A. Wauer, Leipzig, 1900.

edge concerning his activities and those of his missionaries is available: the two Wesley brothers, who were among the converts of the Moravian Church, have described the stages of their conversion for us.[14]

Both brothers had returned from America at the beginning of 1738, sick in body and spirit. John felt himself close to death; Charles came back with a serious case of pleurisy from which he could not recover. Their mission had failed. Their lives had perhaps been wasted. Could they at least testify that they were true Christians? Yes, for they did not believe that they could find peace outside of Christ. No, for despite this belief, they had not succeeded in finding peace *in* Christ. They were worried, afraid, in search of an enlightenment for themselves that they might then share with others.

It was at this point that the Moravian brother Peter Böhler came into their lives. Both Wesleys had already learned to appreciate the evangelical zeal of the Moravians in Georgia. Peter Böhler had been ordained a priest by Zinzendorf the previous year, and since the Church of England had formally recognized the validity of the Moravian episcopacy, John and Charles Wesley did not have the scruples about their relations with him that they might, as Anglican clergymen, have had about similar discussions with an English Dissenter.

Peter Böhler preached justification by faith to them — the faith which, as a free gift of Christ, consists for the individual in believing absolutely that, through the merits of Christ, his sins are forgiven him; a faith which can, just because it was not the fruit of one's own efforts, be secured suddenly, in a moment, by a kind of "instantaneous" miracle. Peter Böhler stationed himself at Charles Wesley's bedside: he moved him, he did not persuade him. He argued with John Wesley and shook him. John knew well that what he lacked in the abyss of despair in which he was submerged was that inner faith

14. See the *Journals* of John Wesley, the *Journals* of Charles Wesley, the *Memoirs of James Hutton.* Also see the biography of Charles Wesley, by T. Jackson; and the biography of John Wesley, by L. Tyerman.

without which works were sterile. On Böhler's instructions he attempted, without yet possessing that faith, to preach the dogma of justification by faith. He achieved sufficient success to disquiet the Anglican clergy and to be refused the right to preach in many London churches. On one point of doctrine — the possibility of instantaneous conversion — John Wesley still hesitated. Böhler sent him back to scripture, and John noted with surprise what he had not perceived until then, that all the conversions reported in the Bible were, in fact, instantaneous conversions. But times had changed. Was it certain that what God had done in the early days of Christianity he wished to repeat today? Replying to this last doubt, Peter Böhler cited "the concordant testimony of many living witnesses." On 25 March at a religious meeting at Blendon, John Wesley, convinced at last, stoutly affirmed the necessity of faith and the instantaneity of conversion. Charles, also present, was indignant, declared the opinions held by his brother "shocking," and rose and left the room.

The same influences nonetheless continued to work upon the two brothers. John had recently abridged and published a new edition of the life of Haliburton, a man of great piety. That very evening of the twenty-fifth, Charles was reading this biography and came across a unique example of instantaneous conversion. He fell ill again, and once more Peter Böhler was at his bedside. At last, on 3 May, Charles was convinced in his turn: like his brother, he believed that to be truly a Christian, one must experience the miracle of faith in one's own soul. On the following day, when Böhler left London and embarked for America, he could say that he had achieved his pious design. Thanks to him, the two brothers awaited the moment when Christ would desire their conversion and grant to them the conviction of salvation, a postponement too full of impatient expectation not to be satisfied in the end. One cannot hover dizzily at the brink of an abyss for three months without eventually stumbling in.

Charles Wesley, always sick, went to live in London at the home of a worker named Bray, a mystic "who has no science but Christ, but who knows and discerns all things by this science." Morning after morning, Charles awoke feverish, hungering and thirsting for Christ but always without Christ. Once again he was in mortal danger. He received the sacraments, "but not Christ." At last, on the evening of Pentecost, having said his prayers and fallen peacefully asleep, he was awakened by a voice which said to him: "By the name of Jesus of Nazareth, arise and believe, and you will be cured of all your ills . . ." The next day, he would learn that he had been the victim of a pious deception. Mrs. Musgrave, a friend of the household, impelled, she said, by an irresistible force, had pronounced the consoling words and worked the long-awaited miracle. "I now found myself," wrote Charles, "at peace with the Lord."

Three days afterward, John Wesley took part in a meeting of a Religious Society in Aldergate Street. Luther's preface to the Epistle to the Romans was being read. "About a quarter before nine," Wesley wrote, "I felt my heart strangely warmed. I felt I did trust in Christ, Christ alone for salvation: And an assurance was given me, that he had taken away *my* sins, even mine, and saved *me* from the law of sin and death."

These two conversions had been awaited, desired, and, as it were, prepared for by the men who underwent them. John Wesley's was so fragile that he was seized by anxiety that very evening and made even more anxious by that very anxiety; how can this renewal of disquiet be explained if he had truly received faith? He consulted a Moravian brother, Telchig, who described to him the theory of Quietism and advised him not to attempt to fight temptation with his own strength but to find refuge "in the wounds of Jesus Christ." He consulted the Gospel of Saint Paul, and for some time consoled himself with a subtle theory which suggested that peace and faith do not necessarily imply joy: "As to the transports of joy . . . God sometimes giveth, sometimes withholdeth them, according to the counsels of his own will."

Later, in recounting the story of his spiritual life, John always tended to understate the importance of this crisis of May 1738. One gets the impression that what gave John Wesley dominance over those who came in contact with him, and his authority over the "Society" which recognized him as its chief, was his stability, the fact that he was not susceptible to sharp emotional upsets. He was not an ecstatic but a man of action. His despair in the spring of 1738 was the despair of an energetic man who had failed in his first designs and was looking for the possibility of new works even as he was preparing his adherence to the dogma of justification by faith without works. At this point the "Germans," Peter Böhler and his associates, intervened. Their instruction helped to "convert" Wesley, to change the direction of his life, by enabling him to discover religious feelings that he had not previously known, feelings that could be translated into action.

Without wasting a moment, he acted. In early June, on Peter Böhler's advice, he established in Fetter Lane, London, after the model of the Moravian societies, the small religious association from which all Methodist churches stem. Then, together with Ingham, one of his old Oxford friends, he left for Herrnhut in Germany, the holy town from which illumination had come to him. By September he was back in London. Then, through the voice of John Wesley and through the voices of his brother, Ingham, and Whitefield, who returned from America at this time, the new preaching burst forth, scandalizing the parish churches and the Religious Societies. The little group of Methodists came together to spend the night of 31 December in meditation, prayer, and ecstasy: 1739, the great year of Methodism, was about to begin.

But for 1739 to be truly the great year of Methodism, for Methodism, having become a popular movement, to inundate the nation, methods of preaching and evangelizing that were then either unknown or repugnant to Whitefield and Wesley were essential. This new discovery, perhaps as decisive in the history of Methodism as the conversion of 1738, can be explained by influences which may still rightly be called foreign. England is not all of Great Britain; for an Englishman of 1740, Ireland, Scotland, and Wales were really foreign countries. These provinces had had a different history from that of England; they had attained a different level of civilization. Though Scotland and Ireland were to be without influence upon the Methodist revival, this was not true of Wales.[15]

15. On the Welsh revival, see T. Rees, *Nonconformity in Wales;* John Rhys and David Brynmor Jones, *The Welsh People,* chap. 10 (details generally

Wales was barely emerging from savagery. The north was inhabited by veritable barbarians, nominally Christians and Protestants, but among whom a mass of superstitious practices of Catholic or even pagan origin persisted. On the south coast the exploitation of the mines was giving rise to industry, and, because of the proximity of Bristol, which made trade easier, civilization began to make some advances. The Nonconformist ministers had made themselves the missionaries of this civilization. It is generally agreed that since 1688 the advance of Nonconformity in Wales had been constant and rapid, while in England Dissent had declined.

The Welsh love exaltation; they have a taste for violent passions. They reproached the Anglican clergymen for being too cold and formal, for appealing to reason rather than to emotion in their sermons. The Nonconformist ministers won hearts; their dogma did not separate religion from religious exaltation; no one in their groups was reputed a Christian until, by a supernatural crisis, God had given him experimental certitude that his sins had been forgiven him. Even in England the preaching of the Welsh Nonconformists had exerted some influence before the coming of Methodism; if the Dissenting sects maintained an incontestable vitality in Northamptonshire, it was because a genuine revival had been underway for about a half-century, under the impetus of two Welsh ministers.[16]

taken from Rees); Hugh J. Hughes, *Life of Howell Harris, the Welsh Reformer;* John Bulmer, *Howell Harris.*

16. On the Northamptonshire revival, which, on a small scale, presents analogies with the Welsh and Methodist revivals, see Thomas Coleman, *Memorial of the Independent Churches in Northamptonshire,* London, 1853. Also see: *A plain and just Account of a most horrid and dismal Plague begun at Rowell, alias Rothwell, in Northamptonshire, which hath infected many places round about,* by Mr. P. Rehakosht . . . , London, 1692; and *An Account of the Doctrine and Discipline of Mr. Richard Davis of Rothwell, in the Country of Northampton . . . ,* London, 1700. On Dissent in Northamptonshire at the beginning of the eighteenth century, see Doddridge, *Free Thoughts,* 1729; *Correspondence and Diary;* John Brime, *A Refutation of Arminian Principles, delivered in a Pamphlet, intitled the Modern Question, concerning Repentance and Faith, examined with Candour . . . ,* 1743 (Cf. Ivimey, *Hist. of the Baptists,* vol. III, p. 270 note).

The Welsh had a further complaint against Anglican clergymen, all of whom preached in English, a language poorly understood in the region. Consequently, the Anglicans were considered foreigners and intruders. The Nonconformist ministers preached in Welsh. Their success persuaded one Anglican clergyman, Griffith Jones, to imitate their method. Like them, he preached in the tongue of his country. Then, outdoing them, he distributed Welsh Bibles and established itinerant schools where children in large numbers learned to read in both languages. But he also submitted to the influence of their beliefs; he learned to understand the dogma of justification by faith, was himself touched by grace, and, once converted, worked conversions. Sincerely attached to the church of which he was a member, he nevertheless made himself suspect to his colleagues both because of the plebeian character of his preaching, and the elated character of his doctrine. Outside his own parish, churches were closed to him. So he preached in private homes and in the open air at church doors. He had lay lieutenants who, at his direction, went all over Wales evangelizing the people. Daniel Rowland was converted by him. From 1735 onward, Howell Harris, his disciple and associate, took over the leadership of this Welsh movement, of which the English movement appears in certain respects to have been only a facsimile.

It should be noted that in the latter months of 1738 the Oxford Methodists, "converted" by the Moravian preachers, had not yet adopted a single one of the techniques which were soon to make Methodism popular. But Whitefield was already corresponding with Howell Harris, who invited him to come and visit him and help him. Whitefield was originally from the West country, on the border of Wales. At the time of his departure for America he had already, three years earlier, preached successfully at Gloucester, his native town. In early February 1739, Whitefield left London; had he not at last yielded to Harris' suggestion?

He arrived in Bristol. Wales supplied this city with wheat, meat, and vegetables, and it was from Wales that Somersetshire recruited a good part of the manpower needed for mining and manufacturing. As soon as he arrived, Whitefield got in touch with the Welsh evangelizers. An interview with Griffith Jones was arranged for him. "More especially," he writes in his *Journal,* "I was edified by the pious Conversation of the reverend *Mr. Griffith Jones,* whom I have desired to see of a long Season. His Words came with Power, and the Account he gave me of the many Obstructions he had met with in his Ministry, convinced me that I was but a young Soldier, just entering the Field." Not content with seeing Griffith Jones, he went beyond the Severn to find Howell Harris at Cardiff, "Whom, though I knew not in Person, I have long since loved in the Bowels of *Jesus Christ* . . . When I first saw him, my Heart was Knit closely to him. I wanted to catch some of his Fire, and gave him the right Hand of Fellowship with my whole heart." It was then that Whitefield began open-air preaching near Bristol among the miners of Kingswood, in the manner of the Welsh preachers.[17]

Whitefield urgently invited John Wesley to come and join him. Wesley arrived on 31 March. He was at first extremely shocked by "this strange way of preaching in the fields." "Having been all my life (till very lately) so tenacious of every point relating to decency and order, that I should have thought the saving of souls almost a sin if it had not been done in a church." His scruples did not last. On 1 April, he spoke indoors to a little Religious Society; but he discussed the Sermon on the Mount and could not refrain from observing that here was "one pretty remarkable precedent of field-preaching, though I suppose there were churches at that time also." On 2 April, he so "demeaned himself" as to preach in the open air before three thousand listeners. Two weeks later, to his great embarrassment, he noted the strange effects of his eloquence: piercing cries, nervous quiverings, fits of fainting. Whitefield had not had such a great effect upon his audience; nevertheless, Wesley had needed all White-field's powers of persuasion to commit this infraction against the established rules and to preach outside of the churches. John Wesley, son of a clergyman, an Oxford man, and a High Churchman, had to overcome prejudices unknown to Whitefield, a former menial at an

17. *A Continuation of the Reverend Mr. Whitefield's Journal, from His Arrival at London to his Departure from thence on his way to Georgia,* London, 1739, particularly 15 January, 22 February, 2 March, 8 March.

inn. That is why Whitefield was not subject to scruples about entering into relations with the authors of the Welsh revival, and of borrowing their methods of preaching — scruples that John Wesley, by himself, might not have been able to overcome.

If the Moravians had not taught Wesley what he must preach in order to capture hearts, would Methodism have come into being? And is it any more likely that Methodism would have come into being if the Welsh preachers had not demonstrated to Whitefield how he must preach in order to give the inception of a sect the aspect and importance of a popular revolution? Methodism consisted in the propagation of Moravian and Welsh enthusiasm in England. Wesley's and Whitefield's good fortune both in London and in Bristol, in 1738 and 1739, was to find themselves precisely where they might be subject to these forces and, consequently, able to transmit them. But the revival had other causes, and we have not yet touched upon the most important of these.

Just as John Wesley's conversion in 1738 under the influence of the Moravian brethren inadequately explains the popular form taken by Methodist preaching in the following spring, so the influence of the Welsh example upon Whitefield does not sufficiently explain the remarkably rapid extension of the movement in England. Why did this idea, which had only made slow progress in Pembrokeshire and Cardiganshire, suddenly create such a sensation in Gloucestershire and Somersetshire, and soon over all of England? Wesley and White-field, to be sure, contributed exceptional gifts of eloquence to the cause for which Griffith Jones, Rowland, and Harris strove in the heart of their province; but may we not presume that they encountered favorable conditions and that their activities took place in a propitious environment? Just at the time when the religious revolution led by Wesley and Whitefield was beginning, a political revolution was underway in England. The simultaneous character of the two events is not, nor could it be, a pure coincidence; it seems that one must have been the effect of the other, or both the effect of an identical cause.

In 1738, after fifteen years of parliamentary dictatorship, the prime minister, Robert Walpole, began to feel his authority threatened. In the course of his long ministry he had disaffected an ever-growing number of parliamentarians. Even within his own Whig party, an opposition had formed with the support or connivance of the Tories. However, it is doubtful that Walpole's opponents would have succeeded in depriving him of his majority in parliament, if they had not been supported by the ever-increasing discontent of public opinion. When Walpole, against his own desire, declared war first against Spain and then against France, he yielded not so much to the threats of parliamentary orators as to the demands of public anger. This complete change of opinion, so long favorable to Walpole, can be explained only by the veritable revolution which England experienced between 1738 and 1745. It is surprising that no historical explanation of this revolution has yet been written.

Since 1688, the country's commerce and industry had been continually growing. England was already moving to the position of the leading mercantile country, workshop, market, and commercial depot of the world; already, English pride delighted in setting forth those triumphant statistics in which, from year to year, may be read the advance in the wealth of the nation. "Normal" progress, Lecky calls it in his *History*,[18] and thus he contrasts it with what he calls the "abnormal," and much more considerable, progress which was achieved at the end of the century after the great mechanical inventions. Certain reservations should be offered concerning this distinction: from the revolution of 1688 until our time, the progress made by English industry will display a greater continuity than Lecky suggested if one takes into account that these great inventions, and the transformation of the industrial order inseparable from them, were themselves the "normal" results of anterior development.

During the first half of the eighteenth century the English merchant had already sought to assure his dominance over the manufacturers whose products he sold. Having established himself in

18. *History of England in the XVIIIth Century,* 1897 edition, vol. I, p. 240. p. 75. Edward [and, later John] Chamberlayne's *Angliae Notitia: of the Present State of England.*

a town, he furnished primary material to the rural manufacturers, buying back from them the manufactured product, with the price being negotiated under almost the same conditions as wages, in our time, are negotiated between the factory owner and his workers. The merchant did not yet own the looms on which the workers labored; but he intended to take possession of their tools and to transform a commercial capitalism into an industrial capitalism. In the silk industry of Derby and in the woolen industry of Yorkshire, ingenious uses of water power anticipated the invention of the steam engine. The industrial era in England dates from 1688, and from the earliest years of the eighteenth century the manufacturing regime presents a great number of characteristics usually assigned exclusively to the regime of "machinofacture."

Pauperism pervaded all the industrial centers, in the manufacturing villages of Wiltshire and Yorkshire, just as it would the huge modern industrial cities a century later. The poverty as well as the ignorance, the immorality, and the intemperance of the working classes were observed and deplored. Timidly, philanthropists attempted to take some action, but their efforts had no effect upon the lower classes. Timidly, statesmen attempted to fight drunkenness by levying excises; they succeeded only in irritating the lower orders, and the parliamentary opposition exploited this irritation. The volumes of Chamberlayne's *Annual* make it possible to measure the degradation of the working classes, which appeared to go hand in hand with industrial advance. "The Day-Labourers, who by their large Wages given them, and the cheapness of all Necessaries," the volume of 1704 reported, "enjoy better Dwellings, Diet, and Apparel in England than the Husbandmen do in many other countries." In the issues appearing around 1740, there is a different story. "The wages of Day-Labourers," the editor wrote at this time, "being but eight or ten pence a Day, in Counties distant from London, those who have large Families find it very difficult frequently to find them Bread."

A commercial crisis would reduce such impoverished workers to complete despair. It is generally held that crises of overproduction did not begin until much later, when steam power and the increase of mechanization had enormously increased the volume of production. However, from the first half of the eighteenth century onward, we see crises analogous to those England would experience a century later, attributable to the same causes and followed by the same results. The first, which broke out in 1738, had a twofold result: it brought about Walpole's fall, and it prompted the eruption of Methodism.

Walpole gloried in a consistently peaceful policy, for which the industrialists and merchants were, for a long while, grateful to him. These classes had not always been hostile to a policy of war. From 1688 to 1712, the Whig party had been the war party, and the mercantile classes had given it electoral and pecuniary support; while Europe was made desolate by war, England, secure from invasion, continued to produce, and consolidated its industrial organization. It took the enormous growth of the national debt, the increase of the tax burden, and the impossibility of finding markets in an exhausted Europe to convert the commercial classes to a peace policy.

In 1738, after more than twenty years of tranquillity, once more finding the disposal of their products difficult, they again became restless and provocative. Shipowners and merchants complained that Spain, to insure its trade monopoly, had secured the right of search on all ships crossing the Atlantic and had profited by thus hindering the commercial relations of England with the New World. Woolen manufacturers, particularly those in the south and the southwest, bemoaning the decline of their industry, attributed this decline to the competition of French manufactures. The metallurgists of Birmingham declaimed against the competition of even the English colonists in America. Their complaints brought on the war with Spain, then with France, and soon would come the time when England, to its misfortune, would provoke a rebellion by the American colonists.

In March 1738, William Pitt gave the signal for attack upon Walpole's peace policy. Some years later, he was to become, in Walpole's place, the master of parliament and of the nation. The Whig party under his leadership would then cease being the party of peace at any price in order to become again, as it had been at the time of William III and Godolphin, the party of all-out war.

At home, Walpole systematically practiced a policy of moral and religious skepticism. Claiming to know the price at which the leaders of political factions might be bought, he made corruption a system of government. Not taking seriously the various theological questions which divided the religious factions, he used his authority on the one hand to place the most rational and skeptical prelates at the helm of the Anglican clergy, and on the other to weaken the virulence of the sects by an affluent and liberal order of things. But political and religious passions were too strong for such a regime to succeed in permanently moderating their ardor. The most telling argument offered by Walpole in defense of his policy was the material prosperity that the nation had enjoyed under his ministry. However, about 1738, industrial and commercial prosperity seemed threatened. The lower orders grew restive. The bestial state to which they had been reduced was seen as putting the social order in jeopardy. Christian philanthropists, denouncing the prevailing state of irreligion, at last roused public opinion. Who, indeed, among Walpole's friends, among the skeptics and freethinkers, had previously been moved by the condition of the working classes?

One of the leading skeptics, Mandeville, in his "Fable of the Bees," had constructed the paradox that the vices of the rich and the ignorance of the poor were a necessary condition for the prosperity of the state. Charity schools, in which the children of the people learned to read the Bible, had been founded. Mandeville decried this, to his mind, criminal and dangerous effort.[19] A half-century later, freethinkers in association with the philanthropists of the evangelical movement would work for the material and moral betterment of the poor. In the interval, they were "converted" to philanthropy through the influence of Methodist preachers. If the bellicose reaction to Walpole's pacifism was personified by William Pitt, the religious and moral reaction to his skepticism was personified by

19. For this controversy, see *A Sermon preach'd in the Parish Church London . . . ,* by John Conybeare, D.D. Dean of Christ Church in Oxford, London, 1788. The speaker, soliciting money for the charity schools, consequently devotes his entire sermon to the refutation of Mandeville.

Whitefield and Wesley. Observe, indeed, the times and places at which the industrial crisis raged; note where the religious crisis burst forth; the evidence demonstrates that the two crises are tied together.

The center of the woolen industry, which would suffer from the crisis more than any other, was, despite the growth of the industry in Yorkshire, still in the flat country extending south of Bristol from the Atlantic coast to the English Channel coast. Today it is a sparsely populated region where cattle graze. Then it was a vast conglomeration of towns, equal in wealth and importance to cities, and of innumerable manufacturing villages where the sheep's wool was no sooner shorn than it was transformed into every kind of cloth, highly prized throughout the world. But the industry went to ruin, and the region was never to lift itself from this crisis. Who was to blame? Was it the government which had allowed the export of contraband English wool, thus supplying the primary materials for continental manufactures? Was it the workers, always agitating, continually conspiring in their workers' associations against the merchants? Their wages were declining; the slightest decrease was enough to make their condition intolerable. Consequently, they accused the merchants of exploiting them and of stealing from them by imposing payment-in-kind in exchange for their work and by even more subtle stratagems. In 1738, uprisings of workingmen took place throughout this region.[20]

Everywhere, day laborers involved in rural manufacturing assembled and marched against the leading industrial towns, where the merchants resided. They plundered, burned; they besieged the homes of merchants, after extorting from them, by threats, a signed undertaking henceforth to give higher pay in exchange for the work of rural manufacturers. In Wiltshire, at Trowbridge, Bradford, and Melksham, the disturbances became so serious that a state of siege was proclaimed, and soldiers were permanently quartered in

20. Nothing, or almost nothing, concerning this crisis can be found either in Macpherson's *Annals of Commerce,* or in Lecky's *History of England,* or in Ashley's economic history, or even in more specialized works, such as John

these localities. In addition to all this, Bristol, the port for the entire region, suffered from still another crisis. The colliery owners of the north of England had formed a syndicate, an "alliance," which had bought up a great number of coal mines, not to exploit them, but rather to diminish the number of producing mines and, by limiting production, to raise prices.[21] This was probably the principal cause of the corn riots which broke out at the end of 1738 among the miners of Kingswood, quite close to Bristol, people well known and much dreaded for the savagery of their ways.

Add to all these things the constant tumult produced by the application of the Gin Act, a virtual riot breaking out each time that an exciseman, in the exercise of his duties, was taken by surprise in a wineshop.[22] "Our mobs," a contemporary wrote, "grow very horrible: here are a vast number of legs and arms that only want a head to make a very formidable body."[23]

James, *History of the Worsted Manufacture,* 1757. To understand its seriousness, however, one need only consult contemporary newspapers (see the leading articles in Boyer's *Political State,* and in the *Gentleman's Magazine*) and the great volume of pamphlets which appeared at that time; especially see *Country Common Sense,* by a Gentleman of Wilts, Gloucester, 1739, a series of essays upon the crisis, which appeared in the *Gloucester Journal,* up to the time the paper refused to continue their publication, probably because their tone was too favorable toward the rebellious workers. They contain a very complete description of the crisis and its causes, and, from our point of view, have a particular interest, since the link between the economic crisis and the Methodist preaching (with which the author reveals a certain sympathy) is clearly stated (Essay 25). The parliamentary opposition also spoke prophetically, both about the impending ruin of the region and the recrudescence of religious passions (Champion, 30 August 1740). Also see the reply of the factory owners to *Country Common Sense: Extracts from the Case between the Clothiers and Weavers and other Manufacturers, with regard to the late Riots in Wilts . . . ,* Gloucester, 1739, and Webber's *Woolen Manufactory,* 1739.

21. Boyer, *Political State of Great Britain,* May 1738, February 1739, April 1739.

22. Ibid., April 1738, September 1738, March 1739.

23. Lady Mary Wortley, *Letters,* vol. II, p. 212, ed. 1837.

It was in this violent atmosphere, in the principal seat of popular unrest, that Methodism was born. The Protestantism of the sectarians had always been influential in this region. It was here that the uprising against the heresy of James Pierce had occurred twenty years earlier. Thus, a throng of small merchants and artisans was prepared to understand the Puritan rallying cries. It was but natural that Christian enthusiasm should endeavor to turn this popular ferment to its own profit. In May 1738, the "French Prophets" appeared.[24] In Bristol, one of their adherents conceived the project of reviving the fervor of the Dissenters, particularly of the very numerous and very influential Quakers. Two "prophetesses," brought from London, went on a Sunday to the Quaker meeting house. Unexpectedly, during the silence of the meeting, one of them rose and threw off her cloak; she revealed herself dressed in a rude sack, her forehead covered with ashes, and hurled forth imprecations. The meeting had to be dissolved. For a few hours, the whole town was in an uproar. In the evening, the sheriff had to send for the soldiery to disperse the mob. This was the prelude to the popular tumult which the Methodist preaching was to bring forth in a great number of English towns.

Eight months after this incident, Whitefield arrived. The Kingswood miners had risen. On 19 January, after the arrest of two of their leaders, the assistance of soldiers was necessary to get the two prisoners away in the face of all the mobbing women and amid a barrage of stones.[25] On 17 February, Whitefield came to Kingswood. "My Bowels," he wrote, "have long since yearned toward the poor Colliers, who, as far as I can find, are very numerous, and yet are as Sheep, having no Shepherd." On the same day he preached a sermon "on a mount" before two hundred listeners. On 21 February, he returned, and two thousand miners listened to him. The movement spread through the entire industrial area of Somersetshire, Gloucestershire, and Wiltshire. Whitefield, both Wesleys, John Cennick, and Benjamin Seward went preaching from town to town.

24. Boyer, August 1739.
25. *Old Common Sense,* 27 January 1739.

Charles Wesley made Bristol his place of residence and the center of his propaganda. The despair of the working class was the raw material to which Methodist doctrine and discipline gave a shape.[26]

The political and economic condition of the country became more and more troubled in the following summer and winter. In vain did Walpole attempt to settle differences with Spain by a peaceful agreement. From the first, the treaty was badly received by the country. Then Spain was accused of not fulfilling its provisions. Public opinion, more and more feverish, demanded war. Finally, in November, Walpole's enemies obtained satisfaction. War was declared. But the war had been ill prepared for, mounted by a pacifist ministry, and began with a series of defeats for England. The economic crisis was exacerbated by the war, a bad harvest, and a very harsh winter. There was a burst of charitable endeavors throughout the nation, and the Methodists took part in organizing relief. When John Wesley opened a weaving workshop near the prayer house he had just built in London, he was merely imitating similar efforts currently being made by others to organize aid by providing work. A well-ordered system of edifying and supportive visits to the poor and sick of the capital produced further recruits to Methodism among the indigent population.

After the southwestern region, Yorkshire was the principal center of the woolen industry. Halifax, Huddersfield, and Wakefield on the Calder River, Bradford and Leeds on the Aire River, and Pontefract at the meeting of the two rivers marked off a region covered, like Somersetshire and Wiltshire, by manufacturing villages; at points, the

26. In order to study this relationship between labor agitation and Methodist preaching in detail, we must become better acquainted with the local history of primitive Methodism than we now are, probably better acquainted than may be possible today. At the end of 1749, for example, there was a labor insurrection at Tiverton serious enough to require the calling of troops, stubborn resistance of the merchants, decay of the region, emigration of many workingmen. In July 1750, we note the arrival of John Wesley and the establishment of a Methodist Society (Martin Dunsford, *Historical Memoirs of the Town and Parish of Tiverton, in the County of Devon*, Exeter, 1790).

West Riding of Yorkshire resembled the outskirts of an immense city. At the beginning of 1739, the crisis was raging there as it had done in the other woolen districts; and it was the generally prevailing poverty that enabled Ingham, a former Oxford Methodist, "converted" by the Moravians at the same time as John Wesley, to produce a revival similar to that of Somersetshire.[27] Having been excluded from the churches in the previous June, Ingham did as Whitefield and Wesley had done at Bristol: he preached in the open air. Then came the winter food shortage. Wheat being extremely expensive, the lower orders rose to seize the wheat which they were unable to buy. At Dewsbury and its surrounding neighborhood, at the end of April, the populace burned down the mills; soldiers were called out; there were dead and wounded.[28] Further north, at Newcastle, the troubles were still more severe. Vessels loaded with grain were pillaged, the town hall was sacked; for a while, the burning of the entire town was feared.[29] These were favorable circumstances for the demonstration of extreme religious ardor.

With the precious assistance of the mason John Nelson – a workingman who had been converted in London by John Wesley and who became one of the greatest lay preachers of Methodism – Ingham founded forty Societies in Yorkshire, which he affiliated to the Moravian church. In 1742, John Wesley, at Nelson's call, traversed the whole of Yorkshire, preaching from one public place to the next, pushing on to Newcastle; in that city and its environs he encountered a mass of workingmen as savage, as degraded, but at the same time as accessible to explosions of collective enthusiasm as the Kingswood miners had been. Newcastle became, with London and Bristol, one of the centers of propagation, one of the "holy cities" of Methodism.

In the southwest, Methodism spread from Bristol and the surrounding countryside to the copper and tin mines of Cornwall, to the coal and lead mines of Wales. In the north, after the initial crisis,

---

27. Tyerman, *The Oxford Methodists,* pp. 109 ff.
28. Ibid., p. 118.
29. *Gentleman's Magazine,* July 1740.

it advanced steadily, in proportion to the needs of the region, as it
developed its industry, for the education and direction of the working class – needs which the state and the established church failed to
satisfy. From Newcastle, Methodism spread through Staffordshire,
Warwickshire, and Lancashire. The very organization that Wesley
imposed on the Methodist Society, which it has kept to our time,
seems to have been based upon the organization of the industrial
society of the time when Wesley went preaching from town to town.
The Wesleyan minister corresponded to the merchant, to the
employer; he was established, as they were, in the central town in
the region, the "circuit." In the surrounding villages, "local
preachers," individual laymen, exerted upon smaller groups of the
faithful an authority comparable to that exercised by the rural
manufacturers, subordinates of the merchants, upon the common
day laborers. In both schemes of organization, the similar hierarchical orders corresponded to the half-urban, half-rural distribu-
tion of the population.

If the explosion in politics and the explosion of religious
enthusiasm came about at the same time, both movements of public
opinion can be traced to the same cause and can be explained by the
same state of popular malaise. We can understand the apprehensions
that the preachings of Whitefield and of Wesley originally inspired.
What religion were the new missionaries going to preach to the
plebeian class of the manufactories? Would not their teachings be
dangerous to the social order and to industrial prosperity? Were not
these Methodists a revival of the Lollards, of the Anabaptists, of the
Levellers? The newspapers gave voice to such fears.

The editor-in-chief of the *Weekly Miscellany* – a hireling defender
of the official church and a bitter enemy of the Methodists – wrote:
If you take the trouble to observe what has generally happened at
the beginning of disturbances which, in the end, have resulted in the
toppling of the constitution and the ruin of the nation, you will be
struck by their resemblance to the upheaval of delirium and enthusiasm which we are witnessing today; if we are not wise enough to
take the necessary precautions in time, there is no doubt but that

there will be fatal consequences. I daresay that today's Enthusiasts have made much more rapid progress, since their first sudden public appearance, than their predecessors made in the same space of time; the nation, today, is more readily disposed to submit to the first evil impulse, to allow itself to be seduced by new ideas, to mistrust authority, and to instigate all kinds of disturbances, than it was when the era of confusion began in the last century.[30]

Common Sense[31] had apprehensions of the same sort: "The labor of the lower classes is the leading source of the prosperity of society. If a solitary individual, like Rev. Mr. Whitefield, has the power, by his preaching, of turning five or six thousand workingmen away from their daily work, what further losses will the public soon suffer? I foresee an enormous increase in the price of coal in the Bristol region, if that gentleman continues his series of charitable meetings among the Kingswood miners." A year later, the *Weekly Miscellany* leveled a more specific charge against Ingham. It reproached him for preaching common ownership of property to the workers who had risen in Yorkshire. Ingham was obliged to deny this charge in a public letter. "If I should admit that I have preached common ownership as this gentleman positively asserts I did, and which I assert I have never done, would it follow that men have the right to pillage, and that they might legitimately seize by force the property of their neighbor? If the second of these propositions necessarily resulted from the first, then the apostles and the early Christians would have been great criminals indeed. . . ."[32] However energetic and sincere Ingham's denials may have been, how can it be denied that his language was of such a nature as to justify, to a certain degree, the mistrust he was trying to dispel. There is in the Gospels too pronounced a messianic element for the governing classes not to be truly alarmed whenever Christian sects advocate a return to primitive Christianity.

30. *Weekly Miscellany,* 12 May 1739.
31. *Old Common Sense,* 19 April 1739.
32. *Weekly Miscellany,* 14 June 1740; answer to the charge published in the 8 June issue.

The Moravians were the initiators of Methodism, and even after the two Wesleys and Whitefield had broken with them, they continued to exert an important influence upon several of their friends, on John Cennick in the southwest, and on Ingham in Yorkshire. The Moravians displayed a deep distaste for violence of any kind; in this, they were as little revolutionaries as were the Quakers; it is equally true that they seem to have envisioned the peaceful transformation of society in the direction of equal shares, and the holding of wealth in common. The colony which they organized at Herrnhut, those which they established at Lamb's Hill in Yorkshire, and the one which, a short time afterward, Howell Harris, inspired by these models, for some time made to flourish in Trevecca in Wales, were small, closed societies, which had at the same time something of the character of a monastery, and a phalanstery. When the Societies founded by Ingham in Yorkshire were dispersed as a result of internal disagreements, a great number of their members passed over to the Scottish sect of "Daleites," named after their leader, Dale, a rich Glasgow industrialist who later became the father-in-law of Robert Owen, and the first initiator of the philanthropic experiments to which Robert Owen was to bring universal repute. Moravianism and Methodism are links in the chain which led from the mystical communism of the Middle Ages to the lay communism of the nineteenth century.

However, the Methodism of Wesley and Whitefield was not to the slightest extent a revolutionary or a communist doctrine. They very rapidly allayed the fears of the governing and commercial aristocracy on this point. Why did the working-class agitation of 1738, after its violent beginnings, take the form of a religious and mystical movement whose ideal was, after all, extremely conservative, rather than terminating in a social revolution? The answer to this question raises difficulties only insofar as one has illusions concerning the role that the common people play in history.

Just because we no longer explain great historical events by citing ministerial decisions, diplomatic intrigues, or the battle plans of generals, there is no reason to move violently to the diametrically opposite conception and to attempt to explain the entire destiny of nations by the blind force of the masses, by the "mystery of crowds." We neglect, between these two forces a singularly influential class, the bourgeoisie, the "middle" class, composed of those who occupy posts of command, high or low, in the economy without participating in the political leadership of the nation, without being members of the governing aristocracy.

The proletariat of the factories and mills, huddled about industrial centers, is accessible to the prompt contagion of all violent emotions. But they are an ignorant mass, not capable of foreseeing and, by themselves, deciding the direction in which their enthusiasm will go. They require a doctrine, an ideal; they need leaders to provide this ideal for them; and these leaders, as a general rule, do not come from the common people. What they possess of culture and knowledge, they owe to a bourgeois education. To whom could the poor appeal in order to find the remedy for their ills if not to those placed immediately above them in the social hierarchy, those from whom they have acquired the habit of seeking help and advice in all the critical circumstances of their lives? It is the bourgeoisie which provides nations with their moral tone.

Imagine, in the England of 1739, a bourgeoisie moved by revolutionary sentiments and convinced that it must instigate a movement of intimidation and insurrection against the existing social order to obtain the satisfaction of its demands. In such circumstances a democratic social revolution could have been brought about. But the English bourgeoisie was not revolutionary. It was not irreligious; the teachings of the freethinkers had only affected the most superficial and most aristocratic segment of the nation. It was not republican; it remembered, with horror and weariness, the disturbances of the preceding century. An economic crisis erupted, the intensity of which was in exact proportion to the immense progress that British industry had made in the preceding half-century. The lower orders in the manufactories were restless. There was the raw material for a general revolt. But popular discontent took the form the discontent of the bourgeoisie wanted to give it: a religious and conservative form. The Methodists were to the Quakers what the latter had been to the Puritans. The Quakers had repudiated the armed republicanism of the Roundheads to the point of displaying an indulgence for the Stuart monarchy, which had disgusted the other Dissenting sects. The Methodists not only declined to identify Protestantism with the doctrine of the right of resistance, but even declined to share the Quaker aversion for every kind of traditional ritual and ecclesiastical discipline. The church they established was at once the most conservative in the political opinions of its members, and the most hierarchical in its internal organization, of all the Protestant sects.

This is how Methodism bent the popular impulses of 1739 to the form which most favored the respect for and maintenance of existing institutions. Even today, whenever a Methodist preacher brings a popular audience together at a street corner to read the Bible, sing hymns, and pray in common, whenever he induces a "revival" of mysticism and religious exaltation, in a region or throughout the nation, the great movement of 1739 is being repeated in the pattern fixed by tradition, with climactic changes of mood that everybody — passionate participants and disinterested spectators — can foresee in advance. A force capable of expending itself in displays of violence or popular upheavals assumes, under the influence of a century and a half of Methodism, the form least capable of unsettling a social order founded upon inequality of rank and wealth.

We do not claim to have written a history of the revival of 1739: we have only tried to show how such a history ought to be written. We have come to the conclusion that the revival was, in the full sense of the term, a historical accident; but we do not mean to suggest by this that it can be fully explained by the natural gifts of two outstanding individuals, John Wesley and George Whitefield.

If two Anglican clergymen, assisted by other clergymen, revived what was left of the Puritan religious sense in the national consciousness, we do not have to see this as a kind of miracle. It was but natural that this would be the case and that the authors of the revival would be Anglican clergymen, not Dissenting pastors. If, furthermore, these clergymen were bound to adopt principles and methods of action which would enable them to act upon the mass of the nation, it was only after they had submitted to foreign and, again, accidental influences, but influences which already presented a certain degree of generality and depth. There were the Protestant refugees who, neglected through the indifference of continental opinion or persecuted through Roman intolerance, avenged themselves by resuscitating the old Puritan ardor on the soil of the nation which had welcomed them. There was the Welsh revival which, leaping over the border, spread to the western counties of England, the least enlightened province thus exercising a kind of contagious influence on the more civilized parts of the nation. But why the unexpected contagiousness of Moravian pietism and Welsh enthusiasm? This, as we have shown, is the point at which the great accident intervened that acted truly decisively on the birth of the Methodist movement.

England experienced a crisis of industrial overproduction of extreme gravity, which reduced the lower orders of the manufactories to poverty and made them accessible to all forms of collective emotion at a time when scientific rationalism had not yet been disseminated among the lowest strata of the bourgeoisie. This is why English Protestantism, suddenly resuscitated and consolidated by this crisis, did not evolve in the direction of philosophic rationalism as among the German Lutherans. This is why in modern England there are no genuine lay parties of social and political revolution. This, in other words, is why after a half-century in which it seemed that free thought must triumph, England reawakened a Puritan nation, and has remained so until our day.

Index